Annual Update

2013

UK Government & Politics

Neil McNaughton

Paul Fairclough

Eric Magee

PHILIP ALLAN

Philip Allan, an imprint of Hodder Education, an Hachette UK company, Market Place, Deddington, Oxfordshire OX15 0SE

Orders

Bookpoint Ltd, 130 Milton Park, Abingdon, Oxfordshire OX14 4SB
tel: 01235 827827
fax: 01235 400401
e-mail: education@bookpoint.co.uk

Lines are open 9.00 a.m.–5.00 p.m., Monday to Saturday, with a 24-hour message answering service. You can also order through the Philip Allan website: www.philipallan.co.uk

© Neil McNaughton, Paul Fairclough, Eric Magee 2013

ISBN 978-1-4441-6888-4

First printed 2013

Impression number 5 4 3 2 1

Year 2016 2015 2014 2013

Typeset by Integra Software Services Pvt. Ltd., Pondicherry, India

Printed by CPI Group (UK) Ltd, Croydon, CR0 4YY

Hachette UK's policy is to use papers that are natural, renewable and recyclable products and made from wood grown in sustainable forests. The logging and manufacturing processes are expected to conform to the environmental regulations of the country of origin.

P02237

Contents

Chapter 1

2012 election round-up: mid-term blues?

Context

The most likely mid-point between UK general elections occurred on 6 November 2012: the next scheduled contest being due on 7 May 2015. Although the collapse of the coalition or a confidence vote carrying the support of two-thirds of MPs could yet bring that election closer, the novelty of a notional 'mid-point' — an otherwise inconsequential spin-off from the Fixed Term Parliaments Act (2011) — offered an ideal opportunity for commentators to reflect on each party's electoral fortunes and assess their prospects.

This chapter provides an overview of the main elections that took place in 2012. In doing so it will answer the following questions:

- What elections took place in 2012?
- Who were the main 'winners' and 'losers' in each of these contests?
- Why did some parties fare better than others: were the coalition partners suffering mid-term blues?

What elections took place in 2012?

Although 2012 saw an absence of what are sometimes referred to as 'first order' elections, there were a number of notable contests nonetheless (see Table 1.1). Significantly, the year also saw the first-ever elections for the newly established Police and Crime Commissioners (PCCs) — contests that are dealt with separately in our end-of-update briefing.

Table 1.1 UK elections in 2012

Type	Details
Parliamentary by-elections	Ballots were held in seven constituencies: Bradford West; Manchester Central; Corby; Cardiff South and Penarth; Croydon North; Middlesbrough; and Rotherham.
London	The election of the mayor of London and the 25-member London Assembly.
Mayoral elections outside London	Mayoral elections were held for the first time in three cities: Bristol; Liverpool; and Salford.
Local elections	Elections in 181 local authorities were held in May: • England: *c.* 4900 seats across 128 authorities. • Scotland: all seats across 32 unitary authorities. • Wales: all seats across 21 unitary authorities.

Who were the main 'winners' and 'losers' in each of these contests?

Parliamentary by-elections

The six by-elections held in November 2012 resulted in few surprises (Table 1.2) apart from the strong showing for UKIP in the ballots held on 29 November. The party came third in one of the contests (Croydon) and second in the other two (Rotherham and Middlesbrough). Labour support (percentage share of the vote) rose in all of these contests (compared with the 2010 general election result), with

Table 1.2 By-elections to the Westminster Parliament, 2012

Election date and constituency		Reason	Result	Turnout	Swing		
					%	From	To
29.3.12	Bradford West	Ill-health	Respect (gain)	50.8%	36.6	Labour	Respect
15.11.12	Manchester Central	Resigned	Labour (hold)	18.2%	16.8	Lib Dem	Labour
15.11.12	Corby	Resigned	Labour (gain)	44.8%	12.7	Conservative	Labour
15.11.12	Cardiff South and Penarth	Resigned	Labour (hold)	25.4%	8.4	Conservative	Labour
29.11.12	Croydon North	Death	Labour (hold)	26.4%	8.0	Conservative	Labour
29.11.12	Middlesbrough	Death	Labour (hold)	25.9%	3.3	UKIP	Labour
29.11.12	Rotherham	Resigned	Labour (hold)	33.6%	7.1	Labour	UKIP

Source: adapted from data in Coleman et al. (2012) *By-elections since 2010*, House of Commons Library Standard Note SN/SG/5833.

support for the coalition partners declining. Although the magnitude of swing in favour of the Labour Party in some of these constituencies (more than 10%) was larger than the average swing towards the party at by-elections held in 2011 (just over 8%), the results were not particularly out of the ordinary for this stage in the electoral cycle.

The result in the seventh by-election, the one held in Bradford West on 29 March, was clearly more significant, as it saw a swing of 36.6% away from Labour, towards the Respect candidate, George Galloway. While it would be easy to dismiss this result as an anomaly caused by nothing more or less than 'the Galloway factor' (a phenomenon last seen in Bethnal Green and Bow in 2005), the result might also be taken as evidence for the view that the Labour Party still has some way to go if it is to re-engage with its core support, specifically, certain ethnic minorities.

Placing the results to one side, the wildly varying turnout witnessed across these seven contests also provoked a good deal of debate. The turnout in Manchester Central, in particular, was one of the lowest on record (see Table 1.3).

Table 1.3 Worst election turnouts

Contest	Turnout
1918 General election	57.2%
2000 London mayoral election	33.7%
1998 Local elections	28.8%
1999 European Parliament elections	24.0%
2012 Police Commissioner elections	18.5%
2012 Manchester Central by-election	18.2%

Source: *Guardian*, 17 November 2012.

Such differences in turnout might easily be explained by considering a number of key variables:
- the circumstances in which each by-election was called
- the nature of each campaign and the appeal of candidates contesting each seat
- the anticipated margin of victory

Manchester Central, for example, is a safe Labour seat where the previous MP (Tony Lloyd) had garnered the support of 52.7% of those who had voted at the 2010 general election. Lloyd, a long-serving constituency MP, had stepped down in order to run in the race to become the inaugural Police and Crime Commissioner for Greater Manchester (a contest which he ultimately won). In short, it was all-too easy for voters in Manchester Central to regard the by-election as something of a 'tidying up' exercise — and one in which the outcome was virtually guaranteed.

In Corby, however, things were very different:
- It was a Conservative seat, offering the prospect of more widespread protest voting.

- The Conservative majority in the constituency at the 2010 general election was under 2000 votes.
- The vacancy resulted from the decision of Conservative MP Louise Mensch — first elected in 2010 — to resign with immediate effect in order to spend more time with her family (a move that had provoked considerable media coverage, not all of it favourable).

London

London mayoral elections operate under the Supplementary Vote (SV) system. Under this method, voters can cast both a first and a second preference. If no candidate secures an absolute majority of first preferences, all but the top two candidates are eliminated and their votes are redistributed according to second preferences (see Table 1.4). At the time that it was introduced, it was felt that the SV system would favour the Labour Party. Many in the party assumed that Labour would always be placed in the top two, alongside the Conservatives, on the basis of first preference votes — and that Labour would do far better than the Tories when the votes of the Lib Dems and other eliminated candidates were transferred according to second preferences. Such assumptions have proved unfounded. In 2000, Livingstone's independent candidacy split the centre-left vote, the result being that the official Labour candidate, Frank Dobson, finished third and was eliminated. Similarly, in 2004, 2008 and 2012, Labour did not benefit from second preference votes to the extent that might have been anticipated.

Table 1.4 London mayoral elections, 2012

Candidate	Party	1st pref.	%	2nd pref.	%	Final Votes	%
Boris Johnson	Conservative	971931	44.0	82880	44.7	1054811	51.5
Ken Livingstone	Labour	889918	40.3	102355	55.3	992273	48.5
Jenny Jones	Green	98913	4.5				
Brian Paddick	Lib Dem	91774	4.2				
Siobhan Benita	Independent	83914	3.8				
Lawrence James Webb	UKIP	43274	1.9				
Carlos Cortiga	BNP	28751	1.3				
Total votes		2208475	100.0	185235	100.0	2047084	100.0

Source: adapted from McGuiness, F. (2012) *London Elections 2012*, House of Commons Research Library Research Paper 12/28.

Aside from Ken Livingstone's defeat — and his subsequent decision to bring the curtain down on a career in frontline politics that has lasted more than three decades — the most notable thing about the 2012 result was, once again, the scale of second preference voting in favour of candidates who had no realistic chance of finishing in the top two on the basis of first preferences.

As we have seen, where no candidate secures more than 50% of first preference voters, the SV system results in the elimination of all but the top two candidates, with their votes being transferred to second preferences. It would make little sense, therefore, for voters to cast their second preferences in favour of parties such as UKIP and the BNP unless they believed that these candidates were likely to finish first or second on the basis of first preference votes.

The fact that both UKIP and the BNP secured significantly more second preference votes (161 252 and 73 353 respectively) than first preferences (43 274 and 28 751) would suggest one of two things:

1 That at least some voters still do not understand how the system works, even after four such elections.

2 That some voters may be using their second preference votes to make a statement (i.e. cast a 'protest vote'), knowing that it will not affect the outcome.

The first explanation is made more compelling by the numbers of spoiled or rejected ballots seen in 2012: 40 210 on first preference and a staggering 445 466 on second preference (though most of the latter had simply been left blank). That said, the 'protest vote' theory might help to explain the performance of several other lower-placed candidates, in particular the Green Party candidate, Jenny Jones, who secured only 98 913 first preference votes, while notionally picking up a further 363 193 votes on second preference.

The elections for the 25-member London Assembly that took place at the same time as the mayoral election produced few surprises (see Table 1.5). Labour, now in opposition at Westminster, increased its share of the vote compared with 2008. The party also increased its tally of seats won from 8 to 12, gaining seats in both the constituency contests (+2 on 2008) and the London-wide seats (again, +2 on 2008). The BNP lost the single seat that it had picked up back in 2008.

Table 1.5 London Assembly seats won, 2000–12 (by party and type)

Party	Total seats won				Constituency seats				London-wide seats			
	2000	2004	2008	2012	2000	2004	2008	2012	2000	2004	2008	2012
Labour	9	7	8	12	6	5	6	8	3	2	2	4
Conservative	9	9	11	9	8	9	8	6	1	-	3	3
Green	3	2	2	2	-	-	-	-	3	2	2	2
Lib Dem	4	5	3	2	-	-	-	-	4	5	3	2
UKIP	-	2	-	-	-	-	-	-	-	2	-	-
BNP	-	-	1	-	-	-	-	-	-	-	1	-
Total	25	25	25	25	14	14	14	14	11	11	11	11

Mayoral elections outside London

2012 saw the election of three new directly elected mayors outside London (see Table 1.6). These mayoral contests, again operating under SV, saw the election of the Independent 'Bristol 1st' candidate, George Ferguson, in an election that had resulted from the May 2012 referendum establishing the post of mayor of Bristol. Although Ferguson failed to secure the 50% of first preference votes required for immediate victory (winning just 35.1% of the popular vote, compared with the second-placed Labour candidate's 29.1%), Ferguson ultimately won a total of 37 353 votes to 31 259, once other candidates had been eliminated and second preferences transferred.

Table 1.6 Mayoral contests, 2012

Date and authority		Turnout	Elected	Party	% 1st preference
03.5.12	Liverpool	30.8%	Joe Anderson	Labour	59.3%
03.5.12	Salford	25.7%	Ian Stewart	Labour	46.0%
15.11.12	Bristol	27.9%	George Ferguson	Independent	35.1%

Local government elections

It is relatively common for the party (or parties) in government to face heavy losses at local elections, even where they continue to perform well at general elections in the intervening years (see Table 1.7). The Conservative Party saw its representation on local councils fall dramatically at the same time that they maintained control at Westminster between 1979 and 1997. New Labour also suffered major losses at local elections in the period 1997–2010. Such outcomes are partly explained by the fact that, where they cast a ballot at all, voters invariably regard such contests as an opportunity to cast a protest vote, a means of sending a message to those in office at Westminster.

Table 1.7 Estimated national share of the vote at local elections (%)*

Year	Conservative	Labour	Lib Dem	Other
2001	33	42	19	6
2002	34	33	25	8
2003	35	30	27	8
2004	37	26	27	10
2005	33	36	23	8
2006	39	26	25	10
2007	40	26	24	10
2008	43	24	23	10
2009	35	22	25	10
2010	37	30	24	10
2011	38	37	16	9
2012	33	39	15	13

* voting figures for general elections are given for those years in which local elections coincided with a general election (shown in italics here)

Source: adapted from McGuiness, F. and Tetteh, E. (2012) *Local Elections 2012*, House of Commons Research Library Research Paper 12/27.

Table 1.8 Local government election results, 2012, in summary

Conservative Party
- 33% of the popular vote
- a net loss of 403 seats
- won or retained control of 42 councils: a net loss of 12
- lost seven councils to no overall control and six to Labour, but gained Winchester from no overall control

Labour Party
- 38% of the popular vote
- a net gain of 823 seats
- won or retained control of 75 councils: a net gain of 32
- won control of six councils from the Conservatives, two Welsh councils from Independents, and 25 councils from no overall control. Lost overall control of Midlothian

Liberal Democrats
- 15% of the popular vote
- a net loss of 330 seats
- the Liberal Democrats retained control of six councils, but lost Cambridge to no overall control

Source: adapted from McGuiness, F. and Tetteh, E. (2012) *Local Elections 2012*, House of Commons Research Library Research Paper 12/27.

In this respect the 2012 local elections again played to type, with Labour making solid gains and the coalition partners — the Conservatives and the Lib Dems — facing significant losses, in terms of both councillors and councils under their overall control (see Table 1.8).

Do local elections matter?

YES

- Such contests offer a useful snapshot of public opinion. They can serve to dissuade the government of the day at Westminster from pursuing certain policies on the national stage.
- Local elections are often significant contests in themselves, in the sense that those public officials returned to office often wield considerable power over those who live within their jurisdictions.
- Such elections allow voters to hold those who set local taxes and determine local expenditure directly accountable.
- Innovations such as the use of STV in local elections in Scotland provide a useful illustration of the way in which different voting systems may contribute to different electoral outcomes.

NO

- Such elections only ever offer a partial — and often unreliable — indication of how parties might fare at a UK-wide general election.

- These contests are often accompanied by high levels of protest voting and worryingly low levels of electoral turnout, thus serving to distort results to an unacceptable degree.
- Under a unitary state, those elected to public office at local level are still ultimately subject to the will of those at Westminster.
- Parties often win back-to-back general election victories, despite suffering massive losses at local elections in the intervening years.

Why did some parties fare better than others: were the coalition partners suffering mid-term blues?

There is little to suggest that the coalition partners performed any worse in these 2012 'mid-term' elections than in the contests held in 2011. In truth, parties in government at Westminster often perform badly in the kinds of contest held in 2012, for the reasons identified earlier in this chapter. While the sheer variety of elections held in 2012 and the considerable variation in outcomes is such that we should probably avoid generalisations on the question of causation, a number of conclusions are becoming increasingly self-evident:

- While Labour has been the chief beneficiary of the public backlash against the coalition's austerity programme, it would appear that the Lib Dems — as opposed to the Conservatives — have suffered most at the polls. This has been particularly apparent in the case of local elections and parliamentary by-elections.
- Though the election of Ed Miliband as Labour leader in place of Gordon Brown has clearly gone some way towards restoring the party's electoral fortunes, results such as the Bradford West by-election would suggest that there is still significant work to be done.
- Labour might have been expected to perform better still, with the economy misfiring and the coalition partners becoming increasingly fractious and eager to delineate their positions ahead of an anticipated general election in 2015.

Summary

- Parties in opposition invariably perform better in second order elections than those in government, due to increased levels of protest voting, tactical voting and low turnouts.
- Labour performed well in six of the seven parliamentary by-elections held in 2012.
- The Labour Party's defeat in the Bradford West by-election suggests that the party still has some way to go before an outright general election victory becomes a realistic prospect.
- Although it lost two of the four mayoral contests held in 2012, Labour made significant gains in the London Assembly elections and in local council elections elsewhere.
- Historically low turnout was an issue in a number of the contests held in 2012.

Exam focus

To consolidate your knowledge of this chapter, answer the following questions:

1 Explain what is meant by the term 'second order elections'.
2 Briefly explain the workings of the SV system employed in UK mayoral elections.
3 How well did the Labour Party perform in the various elections held in 2012?
4 Identify and explain two reasons why opposition parties often seem to perform more impressively in such contests than at general elections.
5 'Voting behaviour at second order elections tells us nothing about the likely outcome of the next general election.' Discuss.

Chapter 2

Political parties: is there a case for state funding?

Context

For many years concern has been expressed in the UK over the way in which political parties are financed. Currently parties are largely financed from the following sources:

- funds raised through special events, mostly at local level
- income from invested funds
- donations from individuals, companies and other associations
- trade unions (the Labour Party largely) through a 'political levy' added to the annual subscriptions paid by members
- some government funding, notably the 'policy grant' divided between larger parties

By far the largest share of funding comes from individual donors, companies and trade unions. It is these sources of finance that have become most controversial. The table below is taken from the Electoral Commission's records of donations to parties in 2011 and shows the scale of this activity.

Party	Donations received in 2011	
	£	Number
Conservative and Unionist Party	14 144 827	758
Labour Party	11 957 097	687
Liberal Democrats	4 131 750	608
Scottish National Party (SNP)	2 820 727	33
Co-operative Party	1 038 316	30
UK Independence Party (UKIP)	325 957	88
Green Party	158 830	30
Plaid Cymru — the Party of Wales	27 067	4

Party	Donations received in 2011	
	£	Number
Scottish Green Party	18 196	2
British National Party	10 000	1
Christian Peoples Alliance	10 000	2
Total	34 642 767	2

Why is party funding controversial?

Since the debate on funding began, a number of issues have arisen which have reinforced the arguments for reform. Among them are these:

- It has long been argued that the funding of the Labour Party by trade unions means that the union movement has exerted too much influence on the party, in particular forcing it to adopt policies on the 'left' of the political spectrum.
- Countering this, it is claimed that the Conservative Party receives a large proportion of its funding from big business and wealthy individuals. Here again, it is claimed to influence policy in such areas as taxation, business regulation and employment legislation.
- It is often claimed that the 'honours system' is corrupted as peerages and other honours may have been granted by party leaders in return for large donations. This is known as the 'cash for honours' system.
- The two main parties have an enormous advantage over the others in terms of raising finance. Naturally, it is argued, donors are likely to support those parties that are more likely to gain governmental power. It seems pointless for them to finance smaller parties that can offer little or nothing in terms of favourable policies.
- There has been concern over the nature of many donors. Some have obtained their wealth in suspect ways, while others may try to hide the 'true' source of the money. Some of these controversial donors are described below.
- Funding and expenditure by parties has grown in recent years, leading to a kind of 'financial race' among the larger parties, with a gradual escalation in spending.
- It is often argued that private donations represent a form of 'secret political influence', even though large donations must be revealed in party accounts.

Some examples of controversial donors

Bernie Ecclestone, head of Formula 1 motor racing, gave £1 million to the Labour Party (originally secretly, though the donation was publicised shortly afterwards) in 1997. Labour, which won the 1997 general election, introduced a ban on sponsorship of sports events by tobacco companies as part of its anti-smoking campaign. When Formula 1 was exempted there was an uproar, with claims that Ecclestone had 'bought' his exemption. The Labour Party was forced to re-pay the donation in 1998.

Lord Ashcroft, a former deputy chairman of the Conservative Party, has donated several million pounds to the Conservatives since the early 1980s. As much of Ashcroft's income was earned abroad he did not pay full UK taxes on it. The donations were therefore claimed to be illegal as they were on foreign, non-taxable earnings, though Ashcroft has claimed they were legitimate. Ashcroft was forced to change his tax status and start to pay UK taxes.

Michael Brown, who donated £2.4 million to the Liberal Democrat Party in 2005, was convicted of serious fraud in 2009. This led to claims that the Liberal Democrats had received some of the proceeds of crime.

Asil Nadir was convicted in August 2012 of stealing many millions of pounds from his own Polly Peck company. Nadir had been a regular contributor to the Conservative Party and so there were calls for his donations to be returned to former shareholders of the bankrupt Polly Peck company.

Trade unions contributed 59% of Labour funds under Gordon Brown, but this had risen to 81% under Ed Miliband by spring 2012 (according to Electoral Commission official figures). This has led to media claims that it is one of the causes of a leftward shift in Labour policy.

Who has called for reform?

There have been three principal sources of possible reform in recent times.

The Committee for Standards in Public Life

The Committee for Standards in Public Life, chaired by Sir Christopher Kelly, is an independent body reporting directly to government. It reported in November 2011 and made three main recommendations:

- There should be a £10000 limit (or 'cap') on any donation by a single individual or organisation.
- £23 million of public funds (on average 50p per voter) should be granted to parties in proportion to the votes attracted by each of them at the last election — broadly this would be £3 per vote won.
- Trade union funding should change. Currently those unions who give money to Labour collect a 'political levy' from their members. This can continue, but the committee recommended that members should have to 'opt in' to paying the political levy, rather than it being deducted unless members 'opt out' as usually occurs presently.

If these reforms were implemented, it is estimated that the parties would receive the funding (shown in Table 2.1) based on the most recent election results.

Table 2.1 Committee for Standards in Public Life: estimated outcome of the proposed reforms in terms of party funding*

Party	Estimated funding (£ million)
Conservative	32.2
Labour	25.8
Liberal Democrat	20.5
Scottish National Party	1.5
Sinn Fein (Northern Ireland)	0.5
Plaid Cymru (Wales)	0.5
Democratic Unionists (Northern Ireland)	0.5

* smaller parties such as UKIP and the BNP would receive some funding for European, London and devolved elections

It can be seen from the figures in Table 2.1 that the main beneficiaries would be smaller parties, especially the Liberal Democrats.

The Parliamentary Select Committee

The Parliamentary Select Committee on Political and Constitutional Reform, chaired by Graham Allen MP, supported the report of the Kelly Committee in January 2012. It urged that there should be cross-party talks to introduce its recommendations after the 2015 election. Graham Allen made the following comments:

> Public concern about party political funding continues to undermine confidence in politics and MPs. It is high time this issue was resolved. The publication of the report of the Committee on Standards in Public Life provides a golden opportunity for the Government to get this issue back out of the box marked 'too difficult' and make a serious effort to find a fair solution which is acceptable to all parties.

Source: www.parliament.uk/business/committees/committees-a-z/commons-select/political-and-constitutional-reform-committee/news/party-political-finance-report/

Contains Parliamentary information licensed under the Open Parliament Licence v1.0.

Unlock Democracy

Unlock Democracy, the pressure group devoted to improving the state of democracy in the UK, supported the Kelly report, while recognising the remaining problems. Unlock Democracy's director, Peter Facey, commented in late 2011:

> We have some sympathy with the proposal that a system of party funding is not affordable under the current political climate and would oppose a system of awarding parties public money on a blanket 'per vote' basis. If the main parties feel that a cap on donations can be introduced without having to dip into the public purse, then we welcome it.

> However, they cannot use it as an excuse not to introduce a cap on donations. Following on from the Liam Fox/Adam Werrity episode, the lines between

lobbying and party funding have never been more blurred. In a time of austerity, it has never been more important that political parties are seen to be serving the interests of the public and not vested interests.

We believe that a case can be made that if a donations cap is set at a low level, for example £10000 per organisation or individual per year, that public money may be required to make up the shortfall. That is up for negotiation; the need for a cap however is not.

Baroness Warsi's [the former Conservative Party chairwoman] claim that money could be better spent on the NHS is unfortunate given that her party is insisting on expensive referendums for elected mayors and direct elections for police commissioners, both of which are of dubious merit and far less crucial than the need to clean up politics in Westminster.

Note: in an interview in the *Sunday Times*, Baroness Warsi said the following on the upcoming report by the Committee on Standards in Public Life:

I fundamentally disagree with [the proposal to give each party £3 for every vote it wins at elections]. At a time when the country is facing the current economic climate, for us to be thinking about putting £100 million, which could build 20 schools and give you thousands of operations on the NHS, into party political funding is wrong. I think people would be appalled by it. They would say, 'That is not what I pay my taxes for'... you would have £1.7 million going to [the British National] party that is going to then push out fascist literature and try to split communities.

Source: unlockdemocracy.org.uk/media/news/entry/parties-must-not-use-opposition-to-party-funding-as-an-excuse-to-block-caps

What are the views of the main parties?

All three main parties have flirted with reform of party funding and supported some kind of change. The main proposals have been as follows:

- **Conservatives** have admitted the need for a cap of £50000 (as opposed to £10000 suggested by the Kelly Committee). In return, however, they want to see reform of trade union donations. They accept Kelly's recommendation that union members should have to express a wish to make a donation to Labour rather than simply having the political levy taken unless they opt out.
- **Labour** leader Ed Miliband suggested in April 2012 that there should be a £5000 cap on individual donations, going even further than Kelly. In a major gamble, he offered to include each trade union within the cap. Individual members would be free to pay a political levy to Labour, but block grants by whole trade unions would not be allowed above £5000. This would severely reduce Labour's source of funding. However, Miliband knows that a £5000 cap would also hit the Tories hard.
- **Liberal Democrats** also support a cap on individual donations, probably along the lines of the Kelly Committee report. They also support the *principle* of some public funding of parties, though on a much more modest scale than Kelly suggested.

- **Small parties** tend to support state funding, especially as they might be the main beneficiaries. However, UKIP rejected the Kelly proposals on the grounds that they would discriminate against small parties. It recommends some state funding, but more evenly spread. The Green Party takes a similar position, as do the nationalists on the whole.
- **The coalition government** has rejected any suggestion of state funding of parties. At a time when there is so much pressure on government finances, such expenditure could not be justified. The Labour Party agrees, though does not rule out state funding at some time in the future. Discussion now largely centres on capping, transparency and the problem of trade union funding of Labour.

Table 2.2 State funding of parties: a summary of the arguments

In favour	Against
• It will reduce the unfair financial advantage enjoyed by the two main parties.	• Taxpayers may object to funding private organisations, especially when there is widespread disillusionment with politicians.
• If fair state funding improves democracy, there is an argument that all should contribute through taxation.	• There are problems over how to allocate funds between parties — should it be based on existing voting support or membership size?
• It will remove the possibility of undue influence exerted by large donors.	
• It will reduce the possibility of hidden donations.	• The funds should be put to better use such as health, education and promoting economic growth.
• It may help to stop the 'escalation' in expenditure by parties on campaigns.	• There is no political consensus over the desirable extent and distribution of funds.
• Most European countries publicly fund their parties so this would bring the UK into line with most modern democracies.	

Summary

- The real question about how parties are funded and whether the state should intervene concerns whether it enhances or threatens democracy. The current situation certainly has few friends, virtually everybody in the political community and the media accepts that the current system is unsatisfactory and undemocratic, but there is widespread disagreement about how to make it more democratic.
- The **undemocratic** features include the fact that there is discrimination against smaller parties and, conversely, there is a major advantage to the large parties. This is because large parties can, naturally, attract more private funding, simply because they are more likely to gain power and so can influence policy. There is a general assumption (though it is often denied by parties and donors) that political funding carries potential influence.

This is only of value if a party is likely to be placed in a decision-making position. The second undemocratic feature is the idea that private donations represent a secret, unaccountable form of influence.

- State funding of parties is considered to be more **democratic** for a number of reasons. First, it would be a transparent system. We would all know where party funding has come from. Second, state funding carries no potential influence. It would be a neutral channel of funds and so would carry with it no hint of secrecy. Third, state funding would reduce the discrimination against small parties. While it is clearly understood that larger parties would, by right, receive more state funding than smaller parties, the current inequalities between the parties could be significantly reduced.

- Though state funding will almost certainly not arrive before 2015, it is such a difficult political issue, with relatively little public support, that it remains a distant prospect. However, there is some possibility that the parties will agree a cap on private donations and reform of trade union donations to the Labour Party.

Exam focus

To consolidate your knowledge of this chapter, answer the following questions:

1 Examine the case for the state funding of political parties.
2 Examine the case against the state funding of parties.
3 Why has the issue of party funding become so controversial?
4 Is the current system of funding political parties undemocratic?

Chapter 3

Coalition economic policy: austerity or growth?

Exam success

The up-to-date facts, examples and arguments in this chapter will help you to produce good-quality answers in your AS unit tests in the following areas of the specifications:

Edexcel	AQA	OCR
Unit 1	**Unit 1**	**Unit F851**
Party policies and ideas	Political parties	Political parties

Context

You will need to have a clear understanding of various key terms that appear in this chapter:

Economic growth is the rise (or fall, when it is known as 'negative growth') in the total value of all goods and services produced in the United Kingdom over a given period of time. The total value is known as **Gross Domestic Product** (GDP). Normally, economic growth figures are calculated each quarter, i.e. every three months. This is used as a general indicator of the health or otherwise of the national economy.

Recession is a term meaning that GDP, as described above, falls in at least *two consecutive quarters.* The data in the next section of this chapter show two recessions — one in 2009 and the other in 2012.

National debt is the *accumulated* debt that is owed by the government (i.e. the country). It arises from all past borrowing that has not yet been paid back. If the government borrows money in one year (which it normally does) this *adds* to the national debt. Sometimes (for example in the late 1990s) the government actually pays back some past debts and does not need to borrow, in which case the national debt is reduced.

Debt interest is the interest that has to be paid on the national debt. Some is paid to members of the public and other organisations that have bought government bonds, which means, effectively, lending money to the government in return for annual interest. The rest is owed to banks, both British and foreign. Interest on the national debt represents a cost to government, which the taxpayer has to bear. It is therefore important that the government can borrow at as low interest rates as possible. Countries with poor credit ratings, such as Greece and Spain, have to offer high interest

rates on borrowing. The UK can borrow at low interest rates because there is confidence we will be able to pay the debts back in due course. This is why such a high value is placed on 'financial responsibility'.

Austerity refers to polices which will reduce the government borrowing burden. This involves reductions in government expenditure, some tax increases on the majority and an acceptance that living standards will fall, at least in the short and medium term.

What was the state of the UK economy in 2012?

The UK entered a recession at the end of 2011 and for the first half of 2012. This was the second recession in three years (see Table 3.1). Both recessions have been characterised as part of the same problem; this is known as a **double-dip recession**.

Table 3.1 Quarterly UK economic growth figures*

Year	Quarter	Rise or fall in GDP
2009	2	−0.6%
	3	−0.2%
	4	+0.4%
2010	1	+0.3%
	2	+1.2%
	3	+0.7%
	4	−0.5%
2011	1	+0.5%
	2	+0.1%
	3	+0.6%
	4	−0.3%
2012	1	−0.3%
	2	−0.4%

* figures in italics represent recession

Source: Office for National Statistics.

The national debt, the total amount owed by the country, is best seen as *a percentage of the Gross Domestic Product (GDP)*. This gives a better indication of how able the country is to service (i.e. pay the interest) on the debt. This can be seen by imagining a household that has total debts, including a mortgage, of £100000. If household income is £50000, then its total debt would be 200% of income. In the same, way we can express total debt as a percentage of GDP for the whole country.

The tables below show how the UK's national debt as a percentage of GDP has changed in recent years and compares this ratio with the state of other economically developed countries.

Table 3.2 UK national debt as a percentage of GDP*

Year	National debt as a % of GDP
1993	34.6
1998	40.0
2006	35.4
2008	38.1
2010	54.8
2012 (estimate)	66.1

* figures *do not* include government spending to support the banking system as this is expected to be repaid in future years. Figures relate to August of each year shown

Source: Office for National Statistics.

Table 3.3 UK national debt as a percentage of GDP and comparisons with other developed countries, 2012*

Country	National debt as % of GDP
France	102.4
Germany	87.3
Greece	181.2
Ireland	118.8
Italy	128.1
Japan	219.1
Spain	77.2
USA	103.6
UK	97.2

* figures here *do* include government spending to support the banking system

Source: OECD.

We can draw a number of conclusions from Tables 3.2 and 3.3:

- Between 1993 and 2008 the total national debt was under control and relatively consistent.
- 2010–12 has seen an alarming rise in the national debt as a percentage of GDP. Although this may appear to be the fault of the coalition, much of the growing debt is a 'hangover' from previous economic and financial policy.
- In comparison with most other economically developed countries, the UK's debt–GDP ratio is not particularly poor, being better than that of France, Japan and the USA and not much worse than Germany's.

Table 3.4 Monthly UK government borrowing
(the so-called 'deficit') — 2010–12 comparison*

August 2010	£11.7 billion
August 2011	£12.7 billion
August 2012	£13.2 billion

* figures show comparison of borrowing in the month of August each year

Source: Office for National Statistics.

Table 3.4 shows that the coalition government has struggled to hold down the government deficit — the difference between what it spends and what it raises in taxation. This is for two main reasons:

1 Many of the expenditure-saving measures and tax increases have not yet 'kicked in'. The effects of those are likely to be seen in 2013 and beyond.

2 The lack of growth in the economy (see Table 3.1 above) has meant that tax receipts have been falling and there have been higher calls on public expenditure in terms of unemployment and other benefits.

Chancellor George Osborne set himself a target. This was to see the national debt fall by 2016. This means he must also eliminate the need for government borrowing within the next few years. The data shown above suggest he will miss his targets by some distance and that he will have to amend them, pushing back the date for the start in reducing national debt.

Is there a trade-off between austerity and growth?

There is a clear trade-off between the need to reduce debt and borrowing, and the goal of economic growth. This is for the following reasons:

■ If austerity measures are adopted, there will be an adverse effect on economic growth. This is basically because the tax rises and reductions in government spending involved will reduce economic activity (for example, consumer spending and industrial investment), so less will be produced.

■ If the government decides to try to stimulate the economy and promote growth by reducing taxation and increasing government expenditure, the deficit will get worse, ultimately resulting in excessively high interest rates, with negative consequences. In the long run, high interest rates will damage economic growth.

■ It therefore seems impossible to achieve *both* growth and austerity.

What are the positions of the main parties on the trade-off?

All three main parties accept that there is a pressing need to reduce government debt. This consensus is broken only by members of the far-left wing of the Labour Party, very much a political minority. The conflicts arise over how the deficit should be reduced and how quickly it should be achieved.

The left

Left-wingers believe the deficit was largely caused by the irresponsible behaviour of the banks. They object strongly to the idea that the whole country, including the less well-off, should have to pay for the mistakes of others. They do not see debt as a major issue and believe that the government should address the issues of poverty, unemployment and inequality. This, they argue, can be achieved despite the deficit as long as taxes are raised on those with the greatest ability to pay, including banks and large companies.

Labour

Labour policy claims that the deficit was largely caused by the world-wide banking system and that reform of the banks is therefore crucial. The deficit does have to be tackled, but over the long term. There should be some short-term reductions in public expenditure, but these must not threaten economic growth. Austerity, the party insists, should largely be targeted at the wealthy and excessive company profits should be taxed to pay off the deficit. The party accepts the need for some 'belt-tightening' and reform of the welfare benefits system, but to a lesser extent than the government.

Conservative

Most, though not all in the party agree that deficit reduction is a priority and that the burden should fall evenly across the whole population. They do not wish to over-tax banks and business for fear of deepening the recession and driving business abroad. Most of the austerity will be accounted for by general reductions in public expenditure including substantial cuts in welfare benefits. They favour some shift in the tax burden towards the middle classes and away from the poor.

Liberal Democrat

The leadership has accepted Conservative deficit-reduction plans, though many party members do not agree. The left-wing elements of the party tend to support Labour policy, while the leaders and moderates have supported coalition policy. Nevertheless they wish to try to shift the burden of taxation towards the rich and away from the poor.

The right

Right-wingers, such as the new Conservative faction, Conservative Voice (see Chapter 6) and UKIP, see deficit reduction as an overwhelming priority for government. They want to see deep cuts in public expenditure, especially on welfare, as well as cuts in taxation, largely corporate taxes, to try to stimulate the economy into growth.

Summary

- The conflict between the need to reduce the financial deficit of government and the need to create economic growth is likely to continue to dominate much of the life of the current parliament.
- It is also probably true that the fortunes of the coalition and its two partners will depend upon how successfully the government is able to handle this difficult trade-off.

Exam focus

To consolidate your knowledge of this chapter, answer the following questions:

1 How do the Conservatives and Liberal Democrats differ on economic policy?
2 How does Labour economic policy differ from that of the coalition government?
3 To what extent is there currently consensus or conflict over economic policy in the UK?

Chapter 4

Directly elected mayors: laboratories of democracy?

Exam success

The up-to-date facts, examples and arguments in this chapter will help you to produce good-quality answers in your AS unit tests in the following areas of the specifications:

Edexcel	AQA	OCR
Unit 1	**Unit 2**	**Unit F852**
Democracy and political participation	Multi-level governance (local democracy)	Constitution (constitutional reform)
Unit 2		
Constitution (reforming the constitution)		

Context

On 6 May 2012, referendums were held in the ten largest English cities where voters had not previously been given the opportunity either to experience local governance under a directly elected mayor or to vote in a ballot to establish one: Birmingham; Bradford; Bristol; Coventry; Leeds; Manchester; Newcastle-Upon-Tyne; Nottingham; Sheffield; and Wakefield. However, only in Bristol did voters deliver a 'yes' vote — with the offer of a directly elected mayor being rejected by significant margins in each of the other nine ballots.

This chapter attempts to put these ten referendums into the broader context of efforts to move towards a more democratically accountable model of English local government. It will consider the position of directly elected mayor — as established initially under the Local Government Act (2000) — while setting aside the separate arrangements established in the capital under the Greater London Authority Act (1999). In so doing it will consider:

- Why were these ten referendums held in May 2012?
- What can we learn from the outcomes of these ballots?
- Laboratories of democracy: has the experiment with directly elected mayors enhanced UK democracy?

Why were these ten referendums held in May 2012?

A pledge to schedule referendums in the 12 largest English cities that had neither balloted residents previously, nor introduced directly elected mayors by some other means, had been included in the Conservative Party's 2010 manifesto (see Box 4.1). In the event, the councils in two of the cities identified in that manifesto

(Liverpool and Leicester) resolved to establish directly elected mayors ahead of the referendums in May 2012, thus reducing to ten the number of cities balloting their residents on 6 May.

Box 4.1 2010 Conservative manifesto

We have seen that a single municipal leader can inject dynamism and ambition into their communities. So, initially, we will give the citizens in each of England's twelve largest cities the chance of having an elected mayor. Big decisions should be made by those who are democratically accountable, not by remote and costly quangos.

Source: adapted from 'Invitation to Join the Government of Britain', p. 76.

Part of a bigger picture?

The Conservative manifesto pledge to kick-start the experiment in directly elected mayors, initiated more than a decade earlier under the Local Government Act (2000), was rooted in the party's 2009 Policy Green Paper No. 9, 'Control Shift: Returning Power to Local Communities'. This document had offered the prospect of a significant transfer of power back from central government and unelected regional quangos, towards locally elected politicians and other directly elected officials (such as directly elected police commissioners, discussed in Chapter 10). The Green Paper had also promised a relaxation of planning laws as part of a raft of measures designed to 'reverse a century of centralisation' with a view to reinvigorating public confidence in — and support for — local democracy. Some commentators expressed the hope that such a shift in power from 'central' to 'local' might even, in time, be matched by a similar shift in the balance of expenditure between the two governmental tiers (see Figure 4.1).

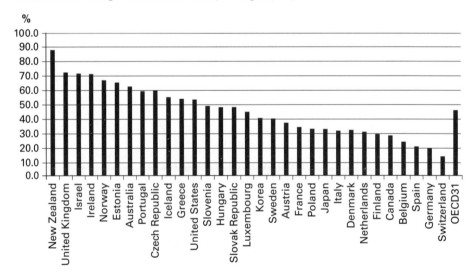

Figure 4.1 Central government expenditure as a percentage of total government expenditure in 2011

The decision to hold these referendums in 2012 can also be seen as a tacit recognition that the long march towards a model of local government incorporating directly elected mayors had lost momentum somewhat, with most of those councils inclined to offer a referendum having already done so. It was hoped that targeting the larger English cities in this way might add fresh impetus to the scheme.

What can we learn from the outcomes of these ballots?

It would be difficult to look at the results of the referendums held in 2012 (see Table 4.1) without arriving at the conclusion that there was little, if any, enthusiasm for the introduction of directly elected mayors in the ten cities targeted. Turnout was universally poor. Even the 'high' of 35.2% in Bradford did little to suggest that what was on offer had inspired local voters, one way or the other. Moreover, Bristol, the only city to return a 'yes' vote, did so on the basis of the second lowest turnout of all (24.1%), with just 53.3% of those who did vote (a shade over one in eight of those who could have cast a ballot) voting 'yes'. Such paltry turnout figures do little to reinforce the democratic credentials of any offices subsequently created (or, for that matter, referendums themselves).

Why was there so little enthusiasm in these ten cities?

The simple answer to the question is that many of those areas enjoying the highest levels of support for directly elected majors had already moved towards this model of executive governance in the wake of the Local Government Act (2000). Another possible explanation of low turnout is the fact that many of those presented with the opportunity to vote in the 2012 referendums clearly either did not understand precisely what difference the change might mean for them in practice, or understood but did not care. This is not an entirely new phenomenon. Those voters who narrowly returned the Hartlepool FC mascot H'Angus the Monkey (aka Stuart Drummond) as the borough's first directly elected mayor back in 2002 were hardly viewing the newly created post with any great reverence.

Coverage of the 2012 referendums would suggest that at least some of those who did cast a ballot, voted 'no' because they feared that a directly elected mayor might wield too much power — or that such posts, where created, would attract mavericks and joke candidates. This view would only have been strengthened by the knowledge that at least a handful of those authorities that had previously adopted the mayoral model were considering abolishing the post. Voters in Stoke-on-Trent did this in 2008 in the wake of a campaign by the Democracy4Stoke group, which branded the mayoral model adopted in the city as 'undemocratic, paternalistic and unsafe'. Indeed, just as voters in the ten cities identified (see Table 4.1) were deciding whether or not to establish new posts, those in Doncaster were voting on whether or not to abolish theirs.

Six months later, in November 2012, voters in Hartlepool went a stage further, abolishing the post of directly elected mayor by a margin of 7366 votes to 5177 on a turnout of just 18%.

Table 4.1 Mayoral referendum results, May 2012

Referendum to establish a directly elected mayor					
City	Outcome	Yes votes	No votes	Turnout	Electorate
Birmingham	No	88085 (42.2%)	120611 (57.8%)	27.7%	754765
Bradford	No	53949 (44.9%)	66283 (55.1%)	35.2%	341126
Bristol	Yes	41032 (53.3%)	35880 (46.7%)	24.1%	318893
Coventry	No	22619 (36.4%)	39483 (63.6%)	26.2%	236818
Leeds	No	62440 (36.7%)	107910 (63.3%)	30.3%	562598
Manchester	No	42677 (46.8%)	48593 (53.2%)	24.7%	369376
Newcastle-Upon-Tyne	No	24630 (38.1%)	40089 (61.9%)	32.0%	202527
Nottingham	No	20943 (42.5%)	28320 (57.5%)	23.8%	206555
Sheffield	No	44571 (35.0%)	82890 (65.0%)	32.1%	397510
Wakefield	No	27610 (37.8%)	45357 (62.2%)	28.3%	257530
Referendum to keep an existing mayor					
City	Outcome	Yes votes	No votes	Turnout	Electorate
Doncaster	Yes	42196 (62.0%)	25879 (38.0%)	30.1%	225796

Source: Sear, C. and Parry, K. (2012) Directly Elected Mayors, House of Commons SN/PC/5000.

Contains Parliamentary information licensed under the Open Parliament Licence v1.0.

Laboratories of democracy: has the experiment with directly elected mayors enhanced UK democracy?

The phrase 'laboratories of democracy' is most commonly used when referring to the form of federalism practised in the USA, where state and local governments are free to experiment and innovate — in effect trialling policies that may subsequently be adopted by the federal (i.e. central) government. As the one-time Supreme Court Justice Louis Brandeis put it in 1932, 'it is one of the happy incidents of the federal system that a single courageous state may, if its citizens choose, serve as a laboratory; and try novel social and economic experiments without risk to the rest of the country'.

To what extent has this laboratories of democracy vision been realised through the innovation of directly elected mayors since 2000?

The reality is that while there was a good deal of enthusiasm for establishing directly elected mayors in the wake of the Local Government Act (2000), there was no meaningful attempt to complete the circle by transferring significant powers away from central government and towards these new, more democratically accountable executives. Instead, the New Labour project saw power centralised or placed in the hands of largely unaccountable quangos, such as the various regional development agencies.

The consequence was that many of the 'first wave' of directly elected mayors inevitably faced the same limitations on their power that had stifled the leadership

Table 4.2 Directly elected mayors excluding the mayor of London (November 2012)

City	Name	Party	Last elected
Bedford BC	Dave Hodgson	Liberal Democrat	2011
Bristol City Council	George Ferguson	Independent	2012
Doncaster MBC	Peter Davies	English Democrats	2009
Hartlepool BC	Stuart Drummond	Independent	2009*
Leicester CC	Sir Peter Soulsby	Labour	2011
Liverpool CC	Joe Anderson	Labour	2012
LB Hackney	Jules Pipe	Labour	2010
LB Lewisham	Sir Steve Bullock	Labour	2010
LB Newham	Sir Robin Wales	Labour	2010
LB Tower Hamlets	Lutfur Rahman	Independent	2010
Mansfield DC	Tony Egginton	Independent	2011
Middlesbrough BC	Ray Mallon	Independent	2011
North Tyneside MBC	Linda Arkley	Conservative	2009
Salford CC	Ian Stewart	Labour	2012
Torbay Council	Gordon Oliver	Conservative	2011
Watford BC	Dorothy Thornhill	Liberal Democrat	2010

*this post will cease to exist in May 2013.
Source: adapted from Sear, C. and Parry, K. (2012) Directly Elected Mayors, House of Commons SN/PC/5000.

Contains Parliamentary information licensed under the Open Parliament Licence v1.0.

committees they had replaced. As the Warwick Commission noted in its 2012 report, 'Elected Mayors and City Leadership', it is probably only now, with the Localism Act (2011) in place (see Box 4.2) and the goal of transferring both power and responsibility to local government established, that the vision of a myriad little laboratories might be realised.

What is needed to deliver local democracy?

While the goal of rebuilding confidence in — and enthusiasm for — local democracy is a laudable one, the recent history of local government reform has been characterised by gimmickry and a penchant for headline-grabbing initiatives. The enthusiasm for directly elected mayors and elected police commissioners could both be seen in this light. However, a similar story was also seen in the case of New Labour's limp efforts to establish directly elected English regional government back in 2004, with voters in the North East referendum apparently unwilling to sanction the creation of a regional assembly that would have operated at considerable expense to local taxpayers, while wielding only limited powers.

Tinkering with the shape and structure of local government is unlikely to deliver the desired outcomes. What is needed is a fundamental shift in power (and money) from central to local institutions. Quite whether or not the Localism Act (2011) will deliver this promised 'control shift' remains to be seen.

Box 4.2 The Localism Act (2011): new freedoms and flexibilities for local government

The Act:

- gives local authorities everywhere the formal legal ability and greater confidence to get on with the job of responding to what local people want
- cuts red tape to enable councillors everywhere to play a full and active part in local life without fear of legal challenge
- encourages a new generation of powerful leaders with the potential to raise the profile of English cities, strengthen local democracy and boost economic growth
- enables ministers to transfer functions to public authorities in cities in order to harness their potential to drive growth and prosperity
- reforms the governance of London so that more power lies in the hands of elected representatives who are democratically accountable to London's citizens

Source: Department for Communities and Local Government (2011), *A Plain English Guide to the Localism Act*.

Crown Copyright. Contains public sector information licensed under the Open Government Licence v1.0.

Summary

- The experiment with directly elected mayors outside London originated with the Local Government Act (2000).
- It was hoped that a single, directly accountable chief executive might be able to provide more dynamic local leadership, while also enhancing greater public confidence in local democracy.
- Ten major English cities held mayoral referendums in May 2012 — though only in Bristol did voters deliver a 'yes' vote. Turnout in all ten contests was low.
- There were 16 such mayors in post by November 2012.
- The goal of reinvigorating local democracy, though laudable, is unlikely to be achieved by changing the structure of local government. Such changes in 'form' need to be accompanied by a shift of 'power' from central to local government.
- It is possible that the Localism Act (2011) might go some way towards delivering this 'control shift'.

Exam focus

To consolidate your knowledge of this chapter, answer the following questions:

1 Why were mayoral referendums held in ten English cities in May 2012?
2 How do directly elected mayors fit into the Conservative Party's broader plans for local government?
3 Does it matter that turnout was so low in these contests?
4 Explain two reasons why most eligible voters either stayed at home or chose to reject the offer of a directly elected mayor in 2012.
5 'Interest and confidence in local government is unlikely to be restored without a new constitutional settlement.' Discuss.

Prime Minister Miliband: no longer an absurd idea?

Context

Ed Miliband's election as Labour leader in 2010 provoked considerable debate. For some commentators it represented the triumph of the union-backed 'Red Ed': a leader who would take the party back to its ideological roots — consigning the New Labour experiment to the dustbin of history. For others, the choice of a former special adviser to Gordon Brown, a man who had 'never had a real job', appeared to promise 'more of the same'. More worryingly for the new Labour leader, few appeared to regard Miliband as a future prime minister. Even many of those in his own party appeared to take the view that the younger Miliband was simply a 'short-term fix', an interim leader who might steer the party through a necessary period of introspection and remodelling in opposition before a more suitable replacement could emerge. In short, Miliband was seen as more of a John Smith, a Michael Howard or a Ming Campbell than a Blair, a Cameron or a Clegg.

This chapter considers whether or not the rather limited expectations that most commentators had of Miliband at the time of his election should be re-evaluated in light of his performance — or the performance of his party — in recent months. In so doing it will consider the following questions:

- Measures of absurdity: what should we use as our yardstick?
- Is Miliband any more likely to become prime minister than he was a year ago?
- Is Miliband any closer to becoming 'prime ministerial' than he was a year ago?

Measures of absurdity: what should we use as our yardstick?

While the proposition offered in the chapter title might, at first, appear clear enough, it should probably be broken down into two separate — if overlapping — questions:

1 Is Ed Miliband likely to become prime minister?

2 Is Ed Miliband likely to become prime ministerial?

The first question obviously hints at a bigger picture: that is, whether or not the Labour Party is likely to have consolidated its position to the extent that it can secure majority control of the Commons at the next general election — or at least emerge as the biggest single party (thus putting Miliband in pole position to become prime minister in a coalition government). Linked to this first question is a supplementary one, namely whether or not Miliband will in fact lead the Labour Party into the next general election campaign.

The second question hints more at the characteristics and qualities now demanded of a UK prime minister. Put simply, the fact that Ed Miliband might become prime minister as a function of his holding the position of Labour leader at a time when the party 'wins' an election does not necessarily make the idea of him taking on the mantle of prime minister any less absurd. After all, Gordon Brown was prime minister — even though many commentators had viewed that eventuality as an absurdity (or at least an aberration) in prospect (i.e. pre-2007), in reality (2007–10), and with the benefit of hindsight (2010 onwards). John Prescott's time as deputy prime minister might easily have been seen in a similar light.

Is Miliband more likely to become prime minister than he was a year ago?

The prospect of Miliband one day becoming prime minister appeared to improve somewhat during 2012. While it is probably fair to say that much of this improvement owed more to the failing economy and a foundering coalition than to Miliband's actions, it would be churlish simply to dismiss his impact on the party's encouraging showings in the polls (see Table 5.1).

Table 5.1 Voting intentions (August–October 2012)

Party	Polling dates		
	24–26 August	20–21 September	19–22 October
Conservative	34%	37%	33%
Labour	39%	38%	41%
Liberal Democrat	15%	14%	14%
Other	12%	12%	12%

Source: ICM Polls for the *Guardian* (figures rounded).

While a 41% share of the vote might not be sufficient to secure an overall majority in the Commons, it would certainly put the incumbent Labour leader in pole position to negotiate with potential coalition partners. Moreover, the absence of any obvious Labour challengers to Miliband's leadership at the mid-point in the electoral cycle would suggest that he is very likely to be in post as party leader at the time of the next general election.

A closer examination of the polling data would, however, suggest that things are not quite so straightforward. For example, while Labour is enjoying a clear lead in the polls, the party still trails the Conservatives on salient issues such as the economy, immigration and Europe (see Table 5.2). Notwithstanding Labour's headline poll lead, the first of these issues (the economy) will clearly be central to the party's electoral prospects once the actual general election campaign begins. While the coalition is itself clearly struggling to kick-start the economy, the reputation for economic competence that New Labour had fought so hard to establish under Blair remains in tatters. Though elections are rarely won and lost on economic issues alone, there are numerous examples of those who have appeared destined to win, ultimately falling short in the face of doubts over their ability to manage the economy (e.g. Labour under Kinnock in 1992).

Table 5.2 Voting intentions and party competence in certain policy areas

Party	Vote for	Best party on...			
		...the economy?	...the NHS?	...education?	...immigration?
Conservative	35%	31	23	27	29
Labour	44%	29	38	32	19
Liberal Democrat	8%	4	6	9	6
Other	13%	4	4	4	12
None	7%	15	13	12	17
Don't know	15%	17	16	16	18

Source: data taken from a YouGov survey conducted 4–5 November 2012.

Is Miliband closer to becoming 'prime ministerial' than he was a year ago?

Irrespective of whether or not Ed Miliband becomes prime minister through leading Labour to victory at the next general election, there is the broader question of whether the idea of him taking on the role of prime minister is itself absurd. While Miliband's 2012 speech at the Labour conference was widely praised, it was essentially an exercise in big-picture mood music. Isabel Hardman in the *Spectator* on 3 October pointed out that it is easy for the party to unite around a speech that deals with the big issues and avoids difficult details of policy. She concluded, 'The far more telling test of Miliband's leadership will be whether

he can steer his party towards policies voters are looking for and make difficult spending decisions while maintaining unity.'

A similar conclusion might easily be drawn from even the most straightforward analysis of the phrases and buzzwords used in the speech itself (see Box 5.1). This was a monologue in which Miliband avoided the fine detail and skirted around some of the more potentially divisive issues for his party (e.g. spending cuts), in favour of positioning himself at the political centre (a 'one-nation' politician) and stressing 'the personal' (i.e. his family).

Box 5.1	**Ed Miliband's 2012 conference speech: the numbers**

Total word count: 7369

- 'One nation' (used 46 times)
- 'NHS' (used 16 times)
- 'My parents', 'my mum', 'my dad' or 'Daniel' — Miliband's son (used 18 times)
- 'Economy' (used 10 times)
- 'Cuts' (used 3 times)
- 'Europe' (used once)

While such an approach might indeed be the way to face down the conference hecklers and win a standing ovation, it will probably take more to convince voters and those on the left of the party that Miliband has what it takes to discharge the duties of prime minister — as opposed to simply occupying the chair. Indeed, a YouGov poll taken on 4–5 November 2012 suggested that the Labour leader still had some considerable way to go in order to win the broader public over to the view that he has 'what it takes' (see Table 5.3).

Table 5.3 Perspectives on the main party leaders

	Party leader		
Characteristic (tick all that apply)	**Cameron**	**Miliband**	**Clegg**
Charismatic	22%	6%	9%
Sticks to what he believes in	18%	19%	7%
A natural leader	17%	6%	4%
Honest	16%	21%	12%
Decisive	14%	11%	4%
Good in a crisis	13%	7%	3%
Strong	13%	9%	3%
In touch with the concerns of ordinary people	7%	26%	11%
None of these	45%	47%	61%
Don't know	8%	13%	12%

Source: adapted from YouGov, 4–5 November 2012.

The 'vision thing'

While this YouGov poll on the leaders of the three main UK parties offered some comfort to Miliband (it is obviously better to be seen as 'honest' and 'in touch', than not), the desperately low figures polled for 'charisma', 'natural leadership', 'strength', and being 'good in a crisis' point straight to the heart of the Miliband conundrum: namely, that two years into his leadership commentators are still struggling to identify precisely what Miliband stands for — and where he might take the country, if given the opportunity to 'lead'.

The big debate at the time of the 2010 Labour leadership contest centred on the question of what direction the party should follow as the New Labour experiment came to its end. The other Miliband (David) had spoken of 'Next Labour' when launching his bid for the leadership. The tabloids gave Ed Miliband the moniker 'Red Ed' when the votes of unions and other affiliates handed him an unlikely victory over his brother in that contest. However, Miliband has hardly promoted an orthodox Red Labour agenda since taking up the reins of the party. Although he has been quick to criticise the coalition's spending cuts, for example, Miliband has conceded that he is unlikely to reverse many (if any) of them. In a similar vein, whereas Miliband has sympathised with public-sector workers, he has stopped short of supporting their decision to take industrial action in defence of their pensions — even going as far as to call such strikes 'wrong'. Miliband has similarly failed to buy into the 'Blue Labour' agenda, despite some attempts to re-connect with the party's core support by taking more conservative positions on Europe and immigration towards the end of 2012.

The Labour leader's failure to articulate a clear philosophy and to 'lead' only serves to bring into sharper focus the concerns of those who from the outset questioned Miliband's right to lead (his brother having won majority support amongst both the parliamentary party and ordinary party members in the original contest: see Table 5.4).

Table 5.4 The 2010 Labour leadership contest

	Electoral college section			
Round 1	**MPs/MEPs**	**Members**	**Affiliates**	**Total**
Abbott	0.88	2.45	4.09	7.42
Balls	5.01	3.37	3.41	11.79
Burnham	3.01	2.85	2.83	8.69
Miliband, D.	13.91	14.69	9.18	37.78
Miliband, E.	10.53	9.98	13.82	34.33
Total*	33.33	33.33	33.33	100.00

Round 2	MPs/MEPs	Members	Affiliates	Total
Balls	5.18	3.83	4.22	13.23
Burnham	3.03	3.30	4.08	10.41
Miliband, D.	14.02	15.08	9.80	38.90
Miliband, E.	11.11	11.13	15.23	37.47
Total*	33.33	33.33	33.33	100.00
Round 3	**MPs/MEPs**	**Members**	**Affiliates**	**Total**
Balls	5.43	4.82	5.77	16.02
Miliband, D.	15.78	16.08	10.86	42.72
Miliband, E.	12.12	12.43	16.71	41.26
Total*	33.33	33.33	33.33	100.00
Round 4	**MPs/MEPs**	**Members**	**Affiliates**	**Total**
Miliband, D.	17.81	18.14	13.40	49.35
Miliband, E.	15.52	15.20	19.93	50.65
Total*	33.33	33.33	33.33	100.00

* totals do not add up owing to rounding of figures

Source: adapted in part from Kelly, R., Lester, P. and Durkin, M. (2010) *Leadership Elections: Labour Party,* House of Commons Library.

The importance of buy-in

As we concluded when assessing David Cameron's prospects in 2010 (see Box 5.2), it is rarely enough in politics to keep quiet on the big issues and hope that one's opponents simply implode. Leaders must, at the same time, engage voters by articulating a positive vision that they can 'buy into': this is what Blair was able to do in 1997; it is what Cameron singularly failed to do in 2010 (much to the chagrin of his fellow Conservative MPs); it is what Miliband needs to do quickly, if he and his party are to avoid falling tantalisingly short of the winning post at the next general election.

Box 5.2 Our assessment of Cameron ahead of the 2010 general election

Though electoral success can be based, to a degree at least, on negative sentiment — a reaction against a party too long in office — it is hard to establish anything of real worth unless one can articulate some kind of coherent vision as to where one wants to take the country. In this respect it is probably fair to say that 'the jury is still out' on Cameron's time as Conservative leader.

Source: *UK Government & Politics Annual Survey 2010.*

Summary

- The apparent absence of serious rivals to Ed Miliband's leadership makes it more likely that he will lead his party into the next general election campaign.
- The fact that the Labour Party is performing relatively well in the polls suggests that Ed Miliband might one day become prime minister.
- Miliband has yet to articulate a clear vision for his party or for the nation.
- Though voters appear to trust the Labour leader, they do not see him as a natural leader.

Exam focus

To consolidate your knowledge of this chapter, answer the following questions:

1 In what ways might the voting intentions polls taken in the autumn of 2012 suggest that Ed Miliband is now well placed to become prime minister?
2 Briefly outline the distinction between 'being prime minister' and 'being prime ministerial'.
3 Explain why the manner of Ed Miliband's election as Labour leader left his mandate to lead the party in question.
4 In what areas, according to the poll findings, would Ed Miliband appear to be lacking?
5 'In office but not really leading.' Evaluate this assessment of Ed Miliband's time as Labour leader.

Chapter 6

David Cameron: a mid-term verdict

Exam success

The up-to-date facts, examples and arguments in this chapter will help you to produce good-quality answers in your AS unit tests in the following areas of the specifications:

Edexcel	AQA	OCR
Unit 2	**Unit 2**	**Unit F852**
The prime minister and cabinet	The core executive	The executive

Context

David Cameron became prime minister in May 2010 under the most unusual of circumstances. By the end of 2012, he will have been in post for just over half his term of office, as the next general election must take place by June 2015 unless, of course, the coalition falls before 2015.

This chapter will examine the performance of David Cameron as prime minister. It is difficult to distinguish between the performance of the government as a whole and that of the prime minister individually, but we will attempt to do so here. We are helped by the fact that Cameron does not try to control all aspects of government, as Margaret Thatcher, for example, attempted to do. For instance, it is clear that education policy is very much in the hands of its minister, Michael Gove. Cameron rarely seems to interfere. The same seems to have been true over welfare reform. The extent to which he concerns himself with economic and financial policy is, however, problematic.

Prime ministerial dominance is easier to analyse when it comes to foreign policy. This is because it is acknowledged within Britain's uncodified constitution that the prime minister has the prerogative power to set and conduct foreign policy.

So, difficult though it may be, we need to evaluate Cameron's performance midway through his first term in isolation from his ministers. Prime ministers are often described as *primus inter pares* (first among equals). We need to judge Cameron on that basis.

Circumstances of Cameron's premiership

Before we judge Cameron we need to remind ourselves of the special circumstances which he has faced since 2010. These include the following.

Negative circumstances

- He lacked authority in that his party had not won the general election.
- He was forced to share power with the Liberal Democrats.
- He has, therefore, limited control over who sits in his cabinet and who should be junior ministers. He must consult with his deputy, Nick Clegg, when replacing departing Liberal Democrat ministers. In other words, he must work with some ministers he has not chosen alone.
- He faces a Parliament where his government's majority is precarious.
- He also faces an active and independent-minded House of Lords.
- He and his government face economic problems, the severity of which few — if any — modern prime ministers have had to deal with.
- Cameron is on the liberal wing of his party and is a moderniser. However, the parliamentary Conservative Party, in both the Commons and the Lords, still contains a large minority of right-wing Conservatives, many of whom remain supporters of radical neo-liberal policies associated with Margaret Thatcher and are also often 'social Conservatives', opposed to social and moral reform.

Positive circumstances

Did Cameron have any special advantages when he took office? This is more difficult to evaluate. We can, however, identify some:

- David Cameron is commonly seen as having a good deal of personal charm and charisma. He handles the media well on the whole (contrast him, for example, with Gordon Brown who was notoriously difficult with the media).
- Although he has had to deal with many problems concerning coalition government, many saw coalition as a potential strength in 2010. At the beginning, at least, the idea of coalition government was viewed optimistically by the public and the media.
- He does command a comfortable majority in the House of Commons, even though the fact that it comes from two parties has created various problems.

How are we to judge Cameron?

The approach we will take is to look at various aspects of his premiership. These are:

- Foreign and defence policy, including how Cameron is seen on the world stage, especially in relation to the European Union.
- Economic policy.
- Social policy and NHS reform.
- Personal standing with the public.
- His ability to control his own government, including his relations with Liberal Democrat ministers.
- His ability to control the Conservative Party in Parliament.

The verdicts

Foreign and defence policy, including how Cameron is seen on the world stage, especially in relation to the European Union

Positives

Cameron was tested early in his premiership when the situation in Libya reached a critical point. In March 2011 the rebel, anti-Gaddafi forces were on the point of defeat. With only days to make a decision, Cameron, along with Barack Obama, was able to secure United Nations' sanction for intervention and despatched RAF elements to enforce a no-fly zone in Libya and to aid the rebels on the ground. The operation was a success with no British casualties and little collateral (i.e. civilian) damage and the rebellion was saved, shortly afterwards removing Gaddafi from power. This was widely seen as a successful intervention, demonstrating both good judgement and decisiveness.

During the financial crisis in the Eurozone, Cameron has played a clever diplomatic game. First, he has successfully resisted any temptation to involve the UK in any significant financial commitments, but at the same time he has had some influence over decision making in the EU. He has steered a course between encouraging the EU to strengthen its fiscal rules to avoid future crises and drawing some strong 'red lines' defining where the UK will not be a party to tighter integration. Thus he has held firm to his party's commitment to preventing any deeper entanglement of the UK with the EU.

Negatives

The UK and Cameron individually have been criticised for their weak stance on the Syrian crisis, but Cameron can argue that, without the support of Russia and China, significant intervention is not possible. Diplomacy has failed, but this can be said for all Western leaders.

Cameron did suffer a degree of embarrassment when he was told by the German and French leaders, Merkel and Sarkozy respectively, to 'butt out' of their plans to save the euro and solve the financial crises in Greece and Spain, on the grounds that the UK does not use the euro.

As part of the general policy of reducing public expenditure, Cameron has sanctioned deep cuts in spending on the armed forces. This has resulted in redundancies from the army and drastic reductions in the UK's naval and air capacity. He has been widely criticised for failing to protect the armed forces at a time when they are particularly stretched.

Summary on foreign and defence policy

Cameron's successes in Libya and in defending the UK's interests in Europe have earned him plaudits. Rather like Tony Blair, Cameron may well be seen more as a dynamic leader abroad than at home.

Economic policy

Positives

Possibly Cameron's greatest triumph at home rests with his achievement, along with George Osborne and Danny Alexander, in putting together a collection of austerity policies to deal with the public deficit. This took place in the face of opposition from elements within his coalition, including the Liberal Democrats and some of his own backbenchers. In contrast with several other European leaders, he has been seen as determined and decisive in this respect.

The danger for the UK in 2010 was that the markets might have seen the country as an unreliable creditor (as has been the case with Spain, Greece and Italy). This might have resulted in the UK having to pay prohibitively high interest rates for its borrowing. Cameron demonstrated a decisive and responsible attitude to tackling the government deficit, so the money markets now lend funds to the UK at very low interest rates.

Negatives

The lack of growth in the UK economy and the recession, which re-emerged in 2012, have largely been blamed on the chancellor, George Osborne. However, Cameron has given his solid backing to Osborne and made it clear he will not backtrack on the deficit-reducing policies, which many blame for the recession. In other words, the recession is seen as a product of Cameron's leadership as much as Osborne's economic policies.

There has also been a good deal of criticism over Cameron's stance on taxation. Having told the nation that 'we are all in this together', he has largely opposed policies that might adversely affect the wealth creators in society and possibly drive some businesses abroad. Some have seen this as a strength, but given Cameron's 'negative' close associations with wealthy individuals, elements of the public and the media have seen this stance as hypocritical.

Summary on economic policy

There is no doubt that Cameron's world standing has been enhanced by his tough position on public expenditure and taxation to deal with the public deficit. At home, however, his support for unpopular policies had begun to affect his position adversely by the end of 2012. As with foreign policy Cameron may be viewed more favourably abroad than in the UK.

Social policy and NHS reform

Positives

Though Cameron has left social policy largely to his ministers, notably Iain Duncan Smith, he has received much credit for his courageous stance on welfare reform. The £26 000 cap on total benefits for each family, reductions in housing benefits and toughening up of the rules for disability benefits have all achieved good public support. They are the kind of policies that have been ducked by past governments on the grounds that they are difficult to achieve. Cameron, however, has backed his ministers and insisted that the reforms must be made. Whether one supports or opposes the changes, his attitude has to be seen as firm and decisive.

On reform of the NHS, Cameron has also proved to be resolute. He supported his beleaguered health secretary, Andrew Lansley (who has since lost his job), during a hugely difficult legislative process during 2011–12 and has succeeded in introducing the *principles* of the reform of the NHS that were developed early in his premiership, although the government was forced to concede many detailed changes.

Negatives

Opponents will argue that David Cameron is likely to go down in history as a prime minister who presided over policies that were divisive and created greater inequality in British society. The effects, they say, of his tax and welfare policies will be to widen the gap between rich and poor. Whether or not this charge is true, and whether the reforms were desirable, is debatable. However, it can be said that David Cameron may have won his arguments within government and in Parliament, but that he has failed to convince the public that Britain will be a fairer society as a result of tax and welfare reforms.

Summary on social policy and NHS reform

It is probably too early to make a judgement on David Cameron in these fields. The effects of the policies will be long term. It is likely that, in years to come, Cameron will be seen either as a determined and successful social reformer, or possibly as a leader who failed to deliver a fairer society. This kind of verdict is remarkably similar to that made on Margaret Thatcher in the 1980s. Her supporters view her as a successful social reformer, while her opponents revile her for presiding over significant increases in inequality.

Personal standing with the public

Positives

Cameron began his term of office well and he out-performed both Nick Clegg and Ed Miliband in terms of public popularity. He also remains slightly more popular, and commands more respect, than his party and the coalition government. In other words, much of the criticism of government has tended to fall on the Liberal Democrats and on George Osborne. Cameron also benefits from being favourably compared with his coalition partner, Nick Clegg.

Negatives

After his promising start, Cameron has now begun to lose the confidence of the public (see *Observer* poll result, Box 6.1 below). Above all, he is increasingly seen as 'out of touch' with ordinary people. He has also been accused of being too 'posh' and, furthermore, of preferring to bring into his government ministers who come from wealthy, privileged backgrounds like his own.

Nadine Dorries, one of his own backbenchers, said in a BBC interview in April 2012 that Cameron and Osborne are surrounded by a tight clique of people who prevent them from understanding what is happening to ordinary people in the UK. She described as their 'real crime' not that they are 'two posh boys who don't know the price of milk', but that they are arrogant, uncaring, and do not *want* to know what other people are experiencing.

Two further criticisms began to be levelled at Cameron during 2012. The first was that he was indecisive and prone to U turns. In particular environmentalists (including London mayor Boris Johnson and his own backbencher, Zac Goldsmith, a prominent environmental campaigner) accused him of 'dithering' over a decision whether to approve the expansion of Heathrow airport. He also allowed George Osborne to reverse a number of unpopular measures in the 2012 budget. The second concerned the revelations of the Leveson Inquiry into press conduct. It was shown that Cameron seemed far too close to a number of discredited journalists and to the Murdoch family.

Box 6.1	David Cameron's personal standing in the polls

In a poll conducted by the *Observer* in September 2012, a representative sample of voters was asked: 'To what extent do you approve or disapprove of the way David Cameron is handling his job as prime minister?' The results were:

Strongly approve:	7%
Somewhat approve:	24%
Neither approve nor disapprove:	16%
Somewhat disapprove:	21%
Strongly disapprove:	31%

The levels of net approval/disapproval for the three main party leaders as shown in the poll were as follows:

Cameron's net disapproval:	−20%
Miliband's net disapproval:	−14%
Clegg's net disapproval:	−48%

Source: *Observer* Opinion Poll, 23 September 2012.

Summary on his personal standing

Cameron's standing with the public and the media is undoubtedly on the wane (Box 6.1). Improvements in the economic performance of the country may help, but there is increasing concern that he is becoming an electoral liability. The contrast with the high regard for Boris Johnson, his potential rival for power, is now striking.

His ability to control his own government, including his relations with Liberal Democrat ministers

Positives

Cameron scores highly in this regard. He has held the coalition together well and there have been no major ministerial resignations over policy conflicts. He has been able to keep together right-wingers in government, moderate Conservatives and Liberal Democrats. Some may argue he has dominated the Liberal Democrats, while others may suggest that he has been effective in persuading worried Liberal Democrats that the government's course of action remains sound. Either way, he has kept together a government that could easily have fallen apart had decisive leadership not been shown. His determination to lead was demonstrated when, in a government reshuffle in the summer of 2012, he removed several moderate Conservatives (notably party chairman, Baroness Warsi) and replaced them with 'right-wingers' (such as new justice secretary, Chris Grayling).

Perhaps his greatest achievement has been to retain Vince Cable as a minister. Cable is on the left wing of the Liberal Democrat party but, by means of a series of minor deals and compromises, he has avoided a damaging resignation by Cable.

Negatives

Although, as we shall see below, some storm clouds may be gathering, Cameron's record as a 'government-unifying prime minister' is almost without flaw. Even when the Liberal Democrat proposals for constitutional reforms collapsed during 2011–12, he kept the Liberal Democrats securely within the coalition.

Summary on his ability to control government

This aspect of Cameron's premiership looks to be the most positive. Cameron and the Conservatives may well lose power in 2015, but, if he can preserve the coalition for five years, it will have been a remarkable achievement.

His ability to control the Conservative Party in Parliament

Positives

The main positive for Cameron is that he has survived intact. He has lost only one major piece of legislation — reform of the House of Lords — and has carried his party and Parliament through a series of problematic economic and social reforms.

Negatives

Serious problems have now arisen. Cameron has lost control of many of his backbenchers twice in recent times. In October 2011, over 80 backbenchers voted in favour of a referendum on Britain's EU membership (a proposal defeated because Labour and the Liberal Democrats opposed it). In July 2012, 92 Conservative MPs defied the whip and Cameron's authority by effectively defeating attempts to reform the House of Lords. This led to severe problems in relations between the coalition partners.

There is also now a new right-wing faction, Conservative Voice (see below), in the party that has begun to threaten his authority.

Summary on his ability to control the Conservative Party in Parliament

Like John Major in 1992–97, David Cameron can no longer rely on his parliamentary majority. His party is split on such issues as immigration, taxation, relations with the EU and welfare policy.

Storm clouds gather

By the end of 2012, Cameron is beginning to look like a beleaguered prime minister. His government is not immediately threatened, but the prospects for the general election of 2015 are looking uncertain. The main problems he now faces as prime minister include:

- A new, right-wing Conservative faction has emerged, known as Conservative Voice. This contains a number of very senior Conservatives, including David Davis, Liam Fox, Priti Patel and Don Porter, its founder. This group represents the views of a significant minority. They stand for such policies as a tougher stance on immigration and the EU, deep cuts in the welfare state to reduce the financial deficit of the government, and cuts in the level of personal and corporate taxes. They complain that Cameron is out of touch, too liberal and too indecisive.
- Boris Johnson is growing in popularity and is perceived as making a success of his mayoralty of London, and there are leaks suggesting he might make a bid for the Conservative Party leadership after 2015.
- The Conservative Party has fallen well below Labour in the opinion polls.
- UKIP is increasingly seen as a threat to the Conservative Party by attracting disaffected members of the party and possibly making a breakthrough in future elections. This will be at the expense of Conservative support. Cameron may well have to concede to UKIP's demands for a referendum on the UK's continued membership of the EU. Such a referendum would split the Conservative Party down the middle with potentially disastrous consequences.
- As the Liberal Democrats dramatically lose public support, they are likely to become more assertive in trying to influence government.
- The economy is failing to respond significantly to attempts to stimulate any growth.

Summary

There are three principles governing the prospects of any British prime minister. These are:

- The state of the economy: it remains the most important factor governing people's political attitude. The poor state of Britain's economy has damaged David Cameron. If the economy improves, it may save him.
- He is at the mercy of events, often beyond his control. Gordon Brown found this. Cameron is, to some extent, at the mercy of economic developments outside the UK.
- The 1960s' Conservative politician, Enoch Powell, said that 'all political careers end in failure'. What he meant was that, as a prime minister's period in office lengthens, the forces of opposition are bound to grow and eventually topple him or her.

David Cameron will be no exception to these truths.

Exam focus

To consolidate your knowledge of this chapter, answer the following questions:

1 What are the main factors that have limited prime ministerial power under David Cameron?
2 To what extent has David Cameron been able to dominate government since 2010?
3 Examine critically the relationship between David Cameron as prime minister and his Parliament since 2010.
4 How has the relationship between the prime minister and the cabinet changed under coalition government?
5 How, and to what extent, has coalition government strengthened or weakened prime ministerial power since 2010?

Chapter 7

The coalition cabinet: is it 'Quad government'?

Context

This chapter is about two developments. One concerns a general assessment of how cabinet government is working under coalition. The second — and this is its main theme — is the apparent trend towards decision making by just four senior ministers. These ministers are reported to be:

- David Cameron, prime minister
- Nick Clegg, deputy prime minister
- George Osborne, chancellor of the exchequer
- Danny Alexander, chief secretary to the treasury (Osborne's deputy)

The media have tended to call this kind of government 'Quad government' (short for quadrilateral) to stress the fact that it involves a very limited 'inner' group, of four people.

Origins of 'inner cabinets'

The use of 'inner cabinets' has a long history. Indeed, we can trace their development back to the early days of cabinet government in the eighteenth century. Small groups of favoured ministers would be gathered round the monarch to make all-important decisions. These policies would then be communicated to other ministers and to Parliament.

It was in the 1960s, however, that the significance of such inner cabinets became apparent. Harold Wilson was the Labour prime minister during 1964–66 and 1974–76. He was a reforming leader and so sought to drive through a number of controversial policies, including the first race relations legislation, equal pay for women, reform of the divorce laws and government regulation of prices and incomes. Wilson knew that, if such policies were left in the hands of the *whole*

cabinet, they would become entangled in arguments over both principles and detail. He therefore tended to operate with a small group of senior ministers (not always the same group).

Since Wilson's day, prime ministers have, to a greater or lesser extent, used inner cabinets to control the policy agenda. When he came to power in 2010, David Cameron suggested that the coalition would signal a return to cabinet government. Cameron assumed that his cabinet would contain such a varied group of politicians from different political backgrounds that he would need to use the whole cabinet to achieve consensus. In reality, however, many commentators suggest that Cameron has had to resort to the traditional device of the inner cabinet in order to control his ministerial colleagues. Before examining this belief we will examine the changed nature of cabinet under coalition.

How does cabinet government work under coalition?

There is a paradox about cabinet government under coalition. Two contradictory developments are apparent.

- On the one hand cabinet has become more important. The need to secure coalition agreement for all new policies has given cabinet a new function. Securing a collective decision on policies can prevent internal divisions within government because all ministers are bound by collective responsibility—the convention that all ministers must support cabinet policy or resign.

- On the other hand cabinet government is weakened by coalition. Taking policy discussions to cabinet carries an immense danger for government. For example the decision whether to concentrate on deficit reduction or whether to promote growth is a divisive issue, especially between Conservatives and Liberal Democrats. The same was true when the NHS reforms were being developed in 2011. Therefore there is a temptation for the prime minister to try to marginalise cabinet. One way of doing this is to develop policy within an inner group and present the cabinet with a *fait accompli*.

Given this paradox, it is remarkable that the coalition cabinet has not suffered a single resignation on the grounds of a policy disagreement. In other words, cabinet tensions have been contained and collective responsibility has been preserved.

Why 'Quad government'?

On Friday, 10 August 2012 David Cameron held a dinner at Downing Street for his three senior colleagues — the so-called 'Quad' of Osborne, Clegg, Alexander and himself. The purpose of the dinner was to reset the coalition after the crisis precipitated by the failure of House of Lords reform and the threat by the Liberal Democrats to retaliate for that failure by blocking government plans to re-draw constituency boundaries — a move that would favour the Conservatives' electoral prospects. There was clearly a fear that the coalition was on the verge of collapse. By drawing together this inner group Cameron was re-asserting its members' determination to make economic growth and deficit reduction key priorities. In doing so, they hoped to restore united, collective government.

Previously, the main function of the Quad had been to establish economic policy. Indeed, before the government budgets were announced in both 2011 and 2012, the Quad was consulted to ensure that there would be no internal conflict over this key area of policy.

What are the main advantages of 'Quad government'?

There are a number of reasons why 'Quad government' can be an advantage to the prime minister:

- The need to deal with the government deficit and the economic recession is so overwhelming that it dominates all other policies. It is therefore logical that the four senior ministers most concerned with deficit reduction and economic recovery should be the central driving force of government.
- The coalition cabinet is potentially very divided. Not only does it contain members from two different parties, it also contains representatives from different *wings* of those parties. There are liberal Conservatives such as Kenneth Clarke (Justice Secretary) and Jeremy Hunt (Culture Secretary), right-wing Tories such as Theresa May (Home Secretary) and Eric Pickles (Local Government and Communities Secretary). From the Liberal Democrats, Danny Alexander and Nick Clegg are centrist moderates, while there are also the more radical left-leaning Vince Cable (Business Secretary) and the neo-liberal Ed Davey (Energy Secretary). Faced with such a disparate collection of powerful ministers, Cameron needs an inner group to be able to dominate the agenda.
- By combining the two leading Conservatives — himself and Osborne — with two of the leading Liberal Democrats — Clegg and Alexander — he hopes to forge a central link between the two coalition partners.

Box 7.1   Tim Montgomerie's ten features of 'the Quad'

Early in 2012, leading Conservative blogger, Tim Montgomerie, identified the following ten features of 'Quad government'. They are:

1. The Quad decides all major matters of policy. This week [February 2012] Cameron, Clegg, Osborne and Alexander have been meeting to discuss what will be in next month's Budget.
2. Downing Street wants us to believe that it's very formal but civil servants aren't always present at its meetings. The Quad met informally over dinner recently, for example.
3. The Quad's power helps explain why the coalition feels like a government that is run by Lib Dems as much as Conservatives. While there are only five yellows [Liberal Democrats] in the cabinet it's not the cabinet that really matters. The yellow team controls half of the votes in the coalition's sovereign chamber.
4. The Quad is deeply political. It is where favours are traded and members are given what they need to keep their respective parties happy. At least up until now that seems to have been pretty much one-way traffic with Cameron and Osborne arranging 'wins' for the Lib Dems. This was especially true after the AV referendum. As Tory unhappiness increases that might change.

5 The Quad isn't just half blue/ half yellow but also half Treasury. 'The Treasury,' concludes James Forsyth, 'is an even greater force in the land than it was in Gordon Brown's day.' Wow. He continues: 'The Treasury fought for decades to get a second cabinet post, finally succeeding in 1961, and even then remained vastly outnumbered in cabinet by ministers from spending departments. Now it has half the people in the room whenever a major decision is taken.'

6 Osborne and Alexander have struck up a particularly good relationship, proving again that people do seem to come under Osborne's spell when they enter his orbit. Contrary to the impression given by TV, Osborne is the more personally charming of the two people at the top of the Conservative Party.

7 The Quad is a happy place. Disagreements are apparently rare. This after all is a meeting of the liberal wing of the Conservative Party and the Orange Book wing [neo-liberal and therefore 'conservative'] of the Liberal Democrats. The social liberals [left of centre] and the Conservative right are not present.

8 The Quad has been watertight until recently but has started to leak. The internal dispute over benefits uprating is the best example of this.

9 The Quad has limited other ministers' freedom to manoeuvre. Decisions taken by the Quad are handed down to other ministers to implement although other ministers are sometimes invited to participate in Quad meetings on a case-by-case basis.

10 The Quad has become a place of compromise rather than grand bargains. At the beginning of the coalition there was a trade of big ideas. For example: 'We get schools reform, you get higher income tax thresholds'... 'We get IDS [Iain Duncan Smith, Conservative] in charge of welfare, you get Huhne [Chris Huhne, Liberal Democrat; since this blog, Huhne has left the cabinet] in charge of energy policy'. That was then — now it's much more about avoiding controversy.

Source: Extract and adaptation of blog by Tim Montgomerie in Conservative Home website. 16 February 2012. http://conservativehome.blogs.com/thetorydiary/2012/02/ten-things-you-need-to-know-about-the-group-of-four-that-runs-the-coalition.html

What are the alternatives to 'Quad government'?

Four other models of cabinet government have emerged under Cameron. In general terms these are:

- That Cameron largely leaves policy making to his **individual ministers** and interferes relatively rarely, and only when special difficulties occur. This has been especially true of Education (Gove), Home Affairs (May), Environment (Spelman) and Welfare (Duncan Smith). He may make speeches on these subjects but leaves policy to the ministers and their departments.

- That most policies are in fact developed in cabinet committees — small groups of senior and junior ministers who consider policy and decisions and then present their recommendations to the whole cabinet for approval. This might be described as '**government by committee**'. The key committees are largely controlled by the prime minister, but others are left to their own devices by David Cameron.

- That Cameron presides over **genuine cabinet government** where important decisions are made collectively. This is an unlikely scenario though the cabinet does, as has been described above, have to reach a collective decision when a policy threatens the unity and survival of the coalition.
- That Cameron adopts a similar style to Tony Blair, known as '**sofa politics**', where he develops policy on a one-to-one basis with ministers outside cabinet and then asks the full cabinet to endorse such plans. 'Quad government' is an expanded form of this applying specifically to economic policy.

It is likely that we will have to wait until David Cameron leaves office before discovering which, if any, of these models is the most accurate.

Summary

- The evidence that cabinet government is, in fact, 'Quad government' remains weak despite Tim Montgomerie's description, given in Box 7.1.
- There is undoubtedly an inner group that meets regularly and tries to maintain a united front. But this group probably only concerns itself with broad economic policy.
- When we scratch the surface there remain fundamental disagreements within the group. For example, Danny Alexander criticises George Osborne for abandoning 'green' economic policies. Clegg is angry about the failure of House of Lords reform on top of the failure of electoral reform. His threat not to co-operate over parliamentary boundary changes has, in turn, angered Cameron.
- Unlike Tony Blair and Gordon Brown, Cameron and Osborne do seem united, but this cannot be said of the relationships between the Conservative and Liberal Democrat members.
- To summarise, therefore, it seems the UK does have 'Quad government' when it comes to economic policy, but this analysis does not hold for any other policy areas.

Exam focus

To consolidate your knowledge of this chapter, answer the following questions:

1 What is an 'inner cabinet' and how does it work?
2 What special problems arise within cabinet as a result of coalition government?
3 Is 'Quad government' little more than prime ministerial government?

Chapter 8

The House of Lords: why is it so difficult to reform?

Context

On 6 August 2012, the deputy prime minister Nick Clegg delivered a Commons statement in which he confirmed that the government would not be seeking to proceed with its House of Lords Reform Bill in the current Parliament — despite the bill having comfortably passed its second reading in the Commons. Such a failure to deliver can have come as no real surprise to those who have charted the course of Lords reform since 1997. Indeed, one might more reasonably be tempted to question why the Liberal Democrat leader had invested so much hope and political capital in an enterprise that was, from the outset, so obviously doomed to failure.

This chapter attempts to explain the failure of the Lords Reform Bill 2012–13, while at the same time addressing the broader question of why the much-heralded second stage of Lords reform has been so hard to deliver. In so doing, it will consider the following questions:

- Was the failure of the bill linked to the nature of its provisions?
- Was there an issue with the bill itself?
- Did the bill fall victim to petty intra-party and inter-party politics?
- Were more deep-seated issues at the heart of this failure?

Was the failure of the bill linked to the nature of its provisions?

It is worth remembering that the bill that was ultimately 'kicked into the long grass' in 2012 had not simply been 'plucked from the air' or 'written on the back of a paper napkin'. It came instead at the end of a concerted cross-party effort, born in the wake of earlier failures. Moreover, the reversal came just two years after a general election campaign in which all three major parties had offered the prospect of significant progress on Lords reform (see Table 8.1).

Table 8.1 Manifesto positions on Lords reform, 2010

Conservative Party	Labour Party	Liberal Democrats
'We will work to build a consensus for a mainly-elected second chamber to replace the current House of Lords.'	'We will ensure that the hereditary principle is removed from the House of Lords. Further democratic reform to create a fully elected Second Chamber will then be achieved in stages.'	'[We will] Replace the House of Lords with a fully-elected second chamber with considerably fewer members than the current House.'

The main provisions of the House of Lords Reform Bill 2012–13 mirrored those of the House of Lords Draft Reform Bill published in 2011 (see *UK Government & Politics Annual Update 2012*). While there was a change to the projected size of the proposed chamber — up from 300 to at least 450 — few who had read the draft bill would have been surprised by the provisions of the bill finally presented to Parliament a year later. The 2012 bill was, in essence, a 'tweaked' version of that draft bill, with the draft bill, in turn, having been a refined version of the White Paper that had run aground in 2007 (see Table 8.2). In short, the 2012 proposals marked the end of an incremental process designed with the sole purpose of addressing those genuine concerns raised at earlier points in the process.

Table 8.2 Comparison between the 2007 White Paper and the House of Lords Reform Bill 2012–13

2007 White Paper	House of Lords Reform Bill 2012–13
The Commons' primacy to be maintained. The Parliament Acts would still apply.	The Commons' primacy to be maintained. The Parliament Acts would still apply.
A reduced chamber of 540 members.	A second chamber of 450 regular members, plus up to 12 Lords Spiritual and additional ministerial members.
A 50:50 split between elected and appointed Lords.	An 80:20 split between elected and appointed Lords — along with an unspecified number of 'ministerial members'.
A single, long, non-renewable term of office.	A single, non-renewable term of 15 years for Lords.
Appointed peers to be selected by a new, independent Statutory Appointments Commission.	90 appointed peers to be chosen by an independent statutory House of Lords Appointments Commission.

2007 White Paper	House of Lords Reform Bill 2012–13
Elected peers to be chosen under a partially open regional party list system.	360 elected Lords to be chosen under a 'partially open', regional list system.
A system of staggered elections, similar to that in the US Senate, with one-third of elected members being chosen at each election.	A system of staggered elections, similar to that in the US Senate, with one-third of elected members (i.e. 120) being chosen at each election.
Elections to coincide with elections to the European Parliament, i.e. every five years.	Elections to coincide with elections to the Commons, i.e. every five years.
20% of Lords to be non-party-political appointees and no party to have an overall majority in the chamber.	The expectation that appointed members would bring a non-party-political perspective to the work carried out by the reformed House of Lords.

Source: 'The House of Lords: Reform White Paper' (CM 7027), February 2007, and the 'House of Lords Reform Bill 2012–13' (House of Commons Research Paper 12/37), July 2012.

Was there an issue with the bill itself?

The substantive concerns that have dogged attempts to complete the second stage of Lords reform can be distilled and presented as three overlapping and interlocking desires:

- a desire to maintain the supremacy of the Commons
- a desire to protect the independence of the Lords
- a desire to guard against a damaging loss of experience and knowledge in the second chamber

To what extent did the bill on offer in 2012 address such concerns?

Maintaining the supremacy of the Commons

The concerns

- Critics of reform had long feared that an elected second chamber might challenge the Commons' primacy.
- It might bring into question the government's mandate to govern.
- A second chamber with its own electoral mandate might even bring into question the Parliament Acts or undermine the Salisbury Convention.
- The existence of elected peers might serve to undermine the existing MP–constituency link.

How did the bill measure up?

- The possibility that the UK might move away from its system of 'asymmetrical bicameralism' towards a more conventional arrangement — where the two legislative chambers would hold co-equal legislative power in a system of 'balanced' or 'symmetrical' bicameralism — was always a red herring.

- The Reform Bill, like the draft bill that went before it, explicitly reiterated the primacy of the Commons, while at the same time preserving the reformed Lords as a 'revising chamber'.
- While it was recognised that the adoption of a regionally based proportional system for elected peers would create constituencies of sorts, there would be no direct challenge to the form of constituency representation offered in the Commons.

Protecting the independence of the Lords

The concern
- Those who favoured a largely appointed chamber argued that the Lords' unelected status made it far easier for peers to discharge their duties and perform as an effective revising chamber — without fear of any electoral backlash.
- The unelected Lords also serves as a barrier against excessive partisanship.

How did the bill measure up?
- Freedom from re-election (with single fixed terms) — as provided for in the bill — would have meant that elected peers would have been free from the need to pander to the electorate.
- The long single term would also have afforded members of the reformed chamber the time and space to develop experience and make a meaningful contribution.
- The expectation that appointed peers would act in a non-partisan manner might also have placated critics — particularly when one considers that 29% of those appointed to the chamber between 1997 and 2012 had previously served as MPs or MEPs and more than 70% of peers take a party whip.

Guarding against a damaging loss of experience and knowledge in the second chamber

The concern
- Opponents of wholesale reform argued that simply sweeping away the remaining 'hereditaries' and life peers overnight in favour of elected replacements would result in a significant loss of legislative experience and competence.

How did the bill measure up?
- The bill proposed a phased reform, with the new elected and appointed peers being introduced in stages over the course of the next three parliamentary election cycles (i.e. 15 years).
- Those favouring such proposals argued that the experience of the existing chamber was, in any case, always overstated. Only 32% of peers in 2012 had served more than 15 years in the chamber — with 52% having been appointed between 1997 and 2010.

In short, there was little in the bill itself that was particularly controversial. Every effort had been made to address the concerns raised at earlier junctures.

Did the bill fall victim to petty intra-party and inter-party politics?

As Nick Clegg conceded in his Commons statement, the government had been forced to abandon the bill not because of a defeat at second reading — the bill had cleared that stage comfortably (462:124) — but because it had become apparent that an unholy alliance of Labour MPs and Tory rebels would make it impossible to secure the 'programme motion' needed for the bill to proceed to the next stage.

Backbench Tory opposition

The Conservatives had enjoyed a healthy in-built majority in the Lords before the first stage of Lords reform in 1999. Though this majority had been surrendered by June 2012 (see Table 8.3), there was still significant resistance to further reform of the Lords on the Tory backbenches. This resistance came both from those who opposed meddling with the constitution in principle and from MPs who thought that there was little to be gained electorally from fiddling with the Lords while the economy crashed and burned.

Table 8.3 Tory strength in the Lords pre-reform and June 2012

	November 1999	June 2012
Conservative	40%	27%
Labour	16%	30%
Liberal Democrat	6%	12%
Crossbench	29%	23%
Other	9%	8%

Source: McGuinness, Feargal, *House of Lords Statistics,* House of Commons Library Standard Note, SN/SG/3900, July 2012.

Mischief-making between coalition partners

Beyond the natural desire of some Conservatives to protect cherished traditions (i.e. to 'conserve'), there was also a sense that the issue offered those backbench Tories frustrated at having been forced into co-habitation with the Liberal Democrats the opportunity to hit their coalition partners where it hurt — by attacking what remained of the programme of constitutional reform re-launched by the Lib Dem leader in the wake of the decisive 'no' vote in the 2011 AV referendum. It was telling, in this context, that Nick Clegg's immediate reaction to the failure of the bill was to announce that the Liberal Democrats would be responding in a 'tit-for-tat' fashion, by withdrawing their support for the agreed boundary changes.

Labour Party politicking

While backbench Tory opposition to the bill presented the government with a significant problem and enflamed simmering tensions within the coalition, it was the position taken by the Labour Party that truly signalled the end of the road for the bill. Though the support of Conservative MPs had, on occasion, carried Blair's New Labour over the line when they sought to introduce policies that were ideologically counter-intuitive (for example, top-up fees and foundation hospitals), Miliband's Labour Party appeared disinclined to help the government by supporting the Lords Reform Bill in 2012 — even though the reform tabled offered the prospect of a second chamber that was not so very far removed from what Labour's own 2010 general election manifesto had envisaged. Labour's contention that they were opposing the programme motion because they believed that yet more time was needed to debate and discuss the bill was viewed with scepticism by those who felt that they had caught the tell-tale whiff of political opportunism. Nick Clegg was certainly forthright in his condemnation of the Labour Party's stated position (see Box 8.1).

Box 8.1 **An extract from Nick Clegg's Commons statement**

In my discussions with the Labour Party leadership, they have made it clear that…while they continue to back Lords reform in principle…they are set on blocking it in practice. Supporting the ends, but — when push comes to shove — obstructing the means. I invited Ed Miliband to propose the number of days that Labour believe is necessary for consideration of the Bill. He declined to do so.... Regrettably Labour is allowing short-term political opportunism to thwart long-term democratic change.

Source: Bowers, Paul, *House of Lords Reform Bill 2012–2013: decision not to proceed*, House of Commons Library Standard Note SN/PC/06405, August 2012.

Were more deep-seated issues at the heart of this failure?

In our 2012 Update we identified and examined a number of long-standing issues that had made the task of executing the second stage of Lords reform such a challenging one. What were these issues and to what extent did they remain 'live' in 2012?

Table 8.4 Long-standing issues affecting the second stage of Lords reform

Issue	Status
A lack of consensus regarding the best way forward.	The lengthy cross-party consultation that led to the final bill was aimed at addressing this very issue. There is little to suggest that many of those still opposing the bill in 2012 were doing so because they had well-grounded concerns that remained unanswered.
The performance of the part-reformed Lords.	The argument that the part-reformed Lords was working well and should be left well alone ('if it ain't broke, don't try to fix it') would also appear to have been debunked, with a number of academic studies making the case for reform on functional/practical — as opposed to simply ideological — grounds.

Issue	Status
Resistance in the Lords, allied to the likelihood that the Parliament Acts could not be used to force through any fundamental change.	Not even an issue in 2012, as the bill never made it to the point where concerted opposition in the Lords might have forced a tactical retreat. Indeed, there is evidence to suggest that the Lords are not, in fact, as averse to reform as they once were: while the Commons were forcing the government to put their plans for Lords reform 'on ice', Lord Steel's House of Lords (Cessation of Membership) Bill — albeit a more modest 'tidying-up exercise' — was able to complete its passage through the Lords on 24 July 2012.

Summary

- The House of Lords Reform Bill 2012–13 was the product of a lengthy process of cross-party consultation aimed at resolving the issues that had led to the failure of earlier initiatives.
- The bill passed its second reading in the Commons with a sizeable majority, only for the coalition to abandon its plans subsequently in the face of opposition to a procedural programme motion.
- Though there are long-standing explanations as to why the much-anticipated 'second stage' of Lords reform has proven difficult to deliver since 1999, most of the arguments explored in earlier Annual Updates cannot readily be applied to the failure in 2012.
- This most recent of failures should probably be attributed more to political opportunism than to issues of substance or high principle.

Exam focus

To consolidate your knowledge of this chapter, answer the following questions:

1 How did the House of Lords Reform Bill 2012–13 differ from the 2007 White Paper?
2 In what ways had the authors of the bill sought to address the concerns raised by earlier critics of Lords reform?
3 Why has it been so difficult to achieve the second stage of Lords reform?
4 To what extent can such longer-term factors be said to have resulted in the failure of the bill in 2012?
5 'If it ain't broke, don't try to fix it.' To what extent do you agree with this view of Lords reform?

Chapter 9

Freedom of information: is it under threat?

Exam success

The up-to-date facts, examples and arguments in this chapter will help you to produce good-quality answers in your AS unit tests in the following areas of the specifications:

Edexcel	AQA	OCR
Unit 2 Judges and civil liberties	**GOVP2** The British Constitution	**Unit F852** The judiciary The constitution

Context

The Freedom of Information Act was passed in 2000 and came into force in stages, the final completion being in 2005. It was part of the constitutional reform programme introduced by the Labour government that came to power in 1997. It was seen as an attempt to bring the UK into line with other modern democracies, most of which had a right to access information enshrined in their laws and/or constitutions. It was also part of a general programme designed to make government more accountable and to introduce the concept of 'open government'.

This chapter will:

- examine the way the Act works
- describe some important examples of how it has been put to use
- report on a number of criticisms that have been levelled at freedom of information in recent years
- evaluate whether there is a possibility that the Act might be repealed or significantly watered down

Background to freedom of information legislation

Above all, without access to information, it was seen as too difficult for Parliament, the media and members of the public to make government and other public bodies accountable for their actions. It had long been thought that government in the UK was too secretive, but it was then also believed that this secretiveness was a threat to individual and group rights. Campaign groups such as Liberty (formerly the National Council for Civil Liberties) and Unlock Democracy (formerly Charter 88) argued that, for true democracy to work effectively, the people must have free access to information about how they are governed.

How does the Freedom of Information Act work?

The Act is quite a complex piece of legislation, but its basic operation is described below. The description can be divided into three parts:

- What rights does it grant?
- What are its limitations?
- What are the powers of the Information Commissioner?

What rights does it grant?

The main rights conferred by the Act are these:

- Any individual citizen has the right to view information held about them by a public body. Public bodies include government, the health service, schools, the tax authorities and financial institutions. In some cases, however, it excludes the police.
- All government papers may be accessed by members of the public or by organisations. This includes papers on policy, decision making, statistics and other information gathered by government departments and agencies. It does not include the exemptions shown below and does not include discussions in the UK cabinet.
- Information held by a wide variety of public bodies is available; the bodies include schools, universities, the police and even some aspects of the armed forces.

What are its limitations?

There are many examples of information that *cannot* be accessed under the Act. However, the main ones include:

- Minutes of cabinet meetings remain confidential for at least 30 years.
- Information related to the *private affairs* of the royal family (though not their public duties).
- The most significant limitation is that there are some pieces of information that cannot be revealed because public knowledge of them would jeopardise the security of the state. These usually involve defence and intelligence issues.
- It is not possible to access confidential information about another person, only about oneself (this was already a restriction under the Data Protection Act, 1998).
- There is a general principle that any information the revelation of which might *not be in the public interest* can be withheld. This is a grey area and often has to be left to judgements by the Information Commissioner (see below for detail of his role).

What are the powers of the Information Commissioner?

The Information Commissioner (currently Christopher Graham) and his office (www.ico.gov.uk) have a number of functions that are vital to the operation of the Freedom of Information Act and the Data Protection Act. The main ones are:

- Giving help to individuals and organisations who wish to access information under the Act.

- Enforcing requests when there is a complaint that the Act is not being complied with.
- Where there is a dispute about whether information should be released — i.e. whether there is a legal justification for withholding the information — the Commissioner will make a judgement on whether the information can be withheld or does not qualify. The most common criteria are: would the information jeopardise state security and would the disclosure be against the public interest? The decisions of the Commissioner are enforceable in law. There is a right of appeal to a judicial tribunal.
- Encouraging the wider general publication of information by public bodies.
- Making reports on the working of the Act and making recommendations for the further publication of information.

Use of the Information Commissioner's powers

MPs' expenses 2008–10 — In February 2008, the *Daily Telegraph* newspaper made a request to see the expenses claims of all MPs and peers. The Information Commissioner allowed the request against strenuous opposition from Parliament and government.

In 2009, the *Daily Telegraph* began to publicise its findings, discovering many examples of claims that were either illegal or at least unjustifiable. It became a major political scandal during 2009–10 with many MPs disgraced. It led to a tightening up of the rules on what MPs and peers could legitimately claim as expenses.

Police records 2012 — In August 2012 a freedom of information ruling forced the Metropolitan Police to reveal 50 million records they were holding about people who had been arrested and questioned, but never charged of an offence. Civil rights groups criticised this decision as it revealed much confidential information about individuals and may 'stigmatise' them even though they have never been charged or tried for an offence. It was argued that this information would aid policing as it would spread intelligence about possible criminals more widely and so help future detection.

Ministers' private e-mails 2012 — In October 2012, the UK government conceded that the private e-mails and texts of ministers, provided they concerned public business, should be released under the FOI Act. This was a victory for the *Financial Times* newspaper that brought the case. It represented significant progress towards more open government.

What do critics of the Act say?

Gus O'Donnell

O'Donnell was cabinet secretary from 2005 to 2011. This made him Britain's most senior civil servant, right at the centre of government, so well placed to observe the working of the Freedom of Information Act at the centre of power.

O'Donnell is a believer in open government and thinks it is best for democracy. However, he criticises the current legislation on a number of grounds:

- Mainly it inhibits ministers, civil servants and advisers from discussing policy *amongst themselves* in an open and honest way. They fear that what they say or write may be revealed in the future and be misunderstood or become the subject of criticism. In other words it has made it more difficult to have confidential discussions within government.
- The Act is too vague and does not make it clear enough what information can be released and what can remain private. In some ways, he claims, important information that could be released is forbidden, while some information ought to remain private. In short the Act needs to be strengthened and made clearer.
- The working of the Act makes it too slow and difficult to access factual information. He would prefer all allowable information to be available to the public routinely, rather than through applications under the Act which can take time and money.
- He wants a new Act that would address these problems.

Tony Blair

In 2012, Tony Blair (prime minister 1997–2007) admitted that he believed a Freedom of Information Act had seemed desirable *before* he came to office in 1997. The experience of being in government, however, had changed his mind. As the extract in Box 9.1 demonstrates, he believes it has hindered government. Ministers and others involved in government have become afraid to discuss policy openly for fear of their thoughts and discussions being too available to the public and especially to the media. The media, he went on, are likely to pursue their own agendas when publicising information.

In general he believes that government can be made more open and more information made available without such an Act, which goes too far towards openness at the expense of secure, confidential consideration of policy.

Box 9.1 Blair on freedom of information

Below is an extract from written evidence given by former prime minister, Tony Blair, to the House of Commons Justice Select Committee as part of its review of the Freedom of Information Act in July 2012.

I am not at all sure that the Act has really achieved its goal of greater transparency. It is essentially used by the media to try to get information that the political system believes should be kept confidential, precisely because it concerns meetings and discussions that are very sensitive. The problem is this: it may well be that those meeting notes and discussions are of great interest. But the truth is that, if people know that what they are saying is going to be published, they will be less frank and open in how they express themselves. If you believe, as I do, that such frankness and openness is essential to the proper conduct of decision-making, then again the impact of publication or even the threat of it, is counter-productive.

continued

The purpose of the legislation was of course not to open such frank discussion to public view. It was to allow issues to be better debated; to permit people to access information about themselves held by Government; and to encourage the system to be more accountable. But if it results in a battle between Government and media — which is really what happens — the way the system will resolve this, is not to continue to fight, but to stop writing things in the same way. I thought the Act would benefit the public. Actually I think it has really tilted the scales on various contentious issues toward the media. Short term that may be fine. Long term it will just result in a different way of conducting the business of Government.

Source: House of Commons Justice Select Committee. 'Post Legislative Scrutiny of the Freedom of Information Act 2000', Written Evidence to the Committee. July 2012. www. publications.parliament.uk/pa/cm201213/cmselect/cmjust/96/tb01.htm

© Parliamentary copyright

Contains Parliamentary information licensed under the Open Parliament Licence v1.0.

David Cameron

Cameron's criticisms of the Act are milder than those of O'Donnell and Blair. He admits that government does find it difficult to make all its information public. He said that it 'furs up' government, meaning that it can slow things down.

However, in March 2012 he told the House of Commons Backbench Liaison Committee that there were no current plans to amend the Act (there were also no plans to strengthen it). Though it did have drawbacks, he said the balance of opinion was that it enhanced democracy and did make government more accountable.

How did the Information Commissioner respond?

Christopher Graham, the Information Commissioner (see also above), replied to these criticisms in a *Guardian* newspaper interview on 16 July 2012. He argued that the Act remained a vital part of Britain's democracy and argued it could be strengthened, not weakened as some politicians have suggested. He also suggested that there were some abuses of the Act, in particular:

- Ministers and advisers were increasingly using private e-mails to avoid their being available to the public under the Act.
- Government documents were being routinely destroyed to prevent their publication.
- Ministers and other officials were increasingly using only verbal briefings when discussing policy, so there would be no documents to be published.
- In many cases private companies are being used to provide government services, especially in the field of welfare, but they are exempt under the Act so the information they hold remains confidential.

In an attack on the critics of the Freedom of Information Act, he said negative comments about the Act by politicians, senior civil servants and media figures were encouraging those lower down the civil service to avoid putting anything in writing. Although Cameron had promised, when he came to power, that his government would be 'the most transparent ever', they were finding freedom of information more difficult to cope with in practice.

What were the findings of the Justice Select Committee Report on the Act?

During 2012 the House of Commons Justice Select Committee conducted a review of the working of the Freedom of Information Act. It took a wide variety of evidence from both government and extra-government witnesses.

On the whole the committee viewed the Freedom of Information Act as a great success. The committee rejected most of the criticisms, including a major attack by Tony Blair. Its chairman, Alan Beith MP, commented in the report:

> The Freedom of Information Act has enhanced the UK's democratic system and made our public bodies more open, accountable and transparent. It has been a success and we do not wish to diminish its intended scope, or its effectiveness. The Act was never intended to prevent, limit, or stop the recording of policy discussions in Cabinet or at the highest levels of Government, and we believe that its existing provisions, properly used, are sufficient to maintain the 'safe space' for such discussions. These provisions need to be more widely understood within the public service.

Source: www.parliament.uk/business/committees/committees-a-z/commons-select/justice-committee/news/foi-report/

© Parliamentary copyright

Contains Parliamentary information licensed under the Open Parliament Licence v1.0.

The coalition government has welcomed the report, suggesting that there is unlikely to be any new freedom of information legislation in the foreseeable future.

Table 9.1 Key benefits and criticisms of the Freedom of Information Act

Benefits	Criticisms
It enhances democracy as people and the media are better informed about the operation of government.	It may inhibit open and frank discussions within government.
It enhances rights as we can discover what information is held about us and can thus correct errors.	It may encourage rather than combat secrecy in government.
It helps to make government and other public bodies more publicly accountable.	It can hinder government and public bodies as a great deal of work may be involved in making information available.
It helps to reveal abuses of power.	Many requests for information are merely mischievous, not serious attempts to reveal key information, and so provide an additional hindrance to administration.

Summary

- Realistically, the Freedom of Information Act is not under threat. As we have seen above, it is strongly supported by Parliament, the public and the media. An attack on freedom of information would be seen as a backward step and a serious blow to Britain's democracy.
- It is an established part of the constitution and a key method by which rights are protected. That it is not popular in governing circles does not mean it is likely to be repealed.
- However, it is possible that there will be calls for its amendment.
- Amendment could move in two directions — either reducing the scope of the Act or increasing it. It may well depend on whether a future government has a right-wing or a liberal complexion.
- Given the recent failure of attempts to amend the UK Constitution (electoral reform, House of Lords changes and reduction in the size of the House of Commons), however, it would seem unlikely that any government would attempt a reform of freedom of information as it would prove to be extremely controversial.

Exam focus

To consolidate your knowledge of this chapter, answer the following questions:

1. What is the Freedom of Information Act and how does it work?
2. Using appropriate illustrations, show how the Freedom of Information Act enhances democracy in the UK.
3. Discuss the main criticisms of the Freedom of Information Act.
4. Assess the strengths and weaknesses of the Freedom of Information Act.

Chapter 10

Briefings

This chapter will bring you up to date with some of the most recent political developments and demonstrate how they are relevant to your studies in government and politics.

Police and Crime Commissioner (PCC) elections: much ado about nothing?

15 November 2012 saw the inaugural elections for Police and Crime Commissioners across England and Wales. In all, 41 posts were up for grabs — one for each force. Elections were conducted under a preferential Supplementary Vote (SV) system of the type used in the election of mayor of London and a number of other mayoral elections nationwide.

Why was this new role established?

The office of PCC was designed to replace the regional police authorities that had existed previously. Those elected to these new positions were to be given the power to steer policing strategy and establish priorities within their regions. Crucially, the PCCs were also to be afforded the right to hire and fire chief constables.

What went wrong?

The elections were blighted by appallingly low turnout across all 41 police areas (see Table 10.1). As a result, a process that was supposed to enhance legitimacy and democratic accountability in policing succeeded in doing neither. The new commissioners, many of whom were elected by narrow margins on record low turnouts, could scarcely lay claim to a far greater mandate than the police authorities they replaced (a fact acknowledged by the former Labour home secretary Charles Clarke in the wake of the results). In short, a process that was widely reported to have cost in excess of £100 million ended in a shambles.

Why did it all turn sour?

The chair of the Electoral Commission, Jenny Watson, blamed the unfamiliar timing of the elections and ministers who had 'made decisions that the commission had disagreed with' (*Guardian*, 17 November). Katie Ghose of the Electoral Reform Society was even less circumspect: 'this is not a reflection of voter apathy', she asserted, 'the public have been given no reason to vote, and no information on either the role or the candidates. This election has been a comedy of errors from start to finish, and those responsible must be held to account.'

Significantly, the published turnout figures in these elections did not include spoilt ballot papers. At recent general elections, the percentage of ballots that are spoilt has generally been around 0.3%. The figures we have for spoilt papers across PCC contests averaged 2.9%. Quite why so many voters spoilt their ballot papers is, of course, open to speculation. The confusion that results when voters face a new electoral system (in this case SV) for the first time often results in incorrectly completed ballot papers. That was certainly true in the first London mayoral election where 2.2% of ballots were spoilt (a figure that had dropped back to 1.8% by 2012). What is clear, however, is that there were at least some voters who deliberately spoilt their ballots because they resented the fact that the campaign had been hijacked by candidates standing on explicit party platforms. We know this much because some voters went so far to set out their concerns (often at great length), in writing, on their ballot papers.

The decision not to fund the cost of candidates sending out mail-shots to voters played into the hands of those candidates who were able to fall back on an established party infrastructure. However, for many voters, the idea of a card-carrying party politician having strategic control over policing was an anathema. It is likely that many of those who chose not to vote on the day were fearful that the process might result in a more politicised police service. However, many of those who did vote were clearly also angry at the efforts of party politicians to snaffle up the new posts, so they actively voted for independents. The result was that independent candidates ultimately secured 12 of the posts available. Such successes were a vindication for candidates such as Martyn Underhill, a former Sussex detective who had launched his ultimately victorious campaign to become PCC in Dorset from his website, **www.keeppoliticsoutofpolicing.co.uk**.

Elsewhere, former deputy prime minister, John Prescott, was thwarted in his attempt to be elected as PCC for Humberside after a campaign which had attracted the attention of the national as well as the regional media. Prescott was quick to apportion blame for his defeat. 'In a normal election, we would have won but, because there were second votes, we didn't', said Prescott (who had also opposed the introduction of the preferential AV system in 2011). 'I can't think of another candidate that had the nationals lining up against them. Only one didn't give me a kicking.'

Table 10.1 PCC election results, 2012 (alphabetically, by force)

Area	Candidate elected	Party	Turnout*
Avon & Somerset	Sue Mountstevens	Independent	18.8%
Bedfordshire	Olly Martins	Labour	17.8%
Cambridgeshire	Graham Bright	Conservative	14.8%
Cheshire	John Dwyer	Conservative	13.7%
Cleveland	Barry Coppinger	Labour	14.7%
Cumbria	Richard Rhodes	Conservative	15.6%
Derbyshire	Alan Charles	Labour	14.4%
Devon & Cornwall	Tony Hogg	Conservative	14.7%

Area	Candidate elected	Party	Turnout*
Dorset	Martyn Underhill	Independent	16.3%
Durham	Ron Hogg	Labour	14.4%
Dyfed–Powys	Christopher Salmon	Conservative	16.4%
Essex	Nicholas Alston	Conservative	12.8%
Gloucestershire	Martin Surl	Independent	16.0%
Greater Manchester	Tony Lloyd	Labour	13.6%
Gwent	Ian Johnston	Independent	14.0%
Hampshire	Simon Hayes	Independent	14.5%
Hertfordshire	David Lloyd	Conservative	14.1%
Humberside	Matthew Grove	Conservative	19.2%
Kent	Ann Barnes	Independent	16.0%
Lancashire	Clive Grunshaw	Labour	15.0%
Leicestershire	Clive Loader	Conservative	16.0%
Lincolnshire	Alan Hardwick	Independent	15.3%
Merseyside	Jane Kennedy	Labour	12.4%
Norfolk	Stephen Bett	Independent	14.5%
North Wales	Winston Roddick	Independent	14.8%
North Yorkshire	Julia Mulligan	Conservative	13.3%
Northamptonshire	Adam Simmonds	Conservative	20.0%
Northumbria	Vera Baird	Labour	16.4%
Nottinghamshire	Paddy Tipping	Labour	16.4%
South Wales	Alun Michael	Labour	14.7%
South Yorkshire	Shaun Wright	Labour	14.5%
Staffordshire	Matthew Ellis	Conservative	11.6%
Suffolk	Tim Passmore	Conservative	15.4%
Surrey	Kevin Hurley	Zero Tolerance Policing	15.4%
Sussex	Katy Bourne	Conservative	15.3%
Thames Valley	Anthony Stansfeld	Conservative	13.3%
Warwickshire	Ron Ball	Independent	15.2%
West Mercia	Bill Longmore	Independent	14.5%
West Midlands	Bob Jones	Labour	12.0%
West Yorkshire	Mark Burns-Williamson	Labour	13.3%
Wiltshire	Angus MacPherson	Conservative	15.3%

*turnout figures do not include spoilt ballot papers

MacShane: yet another casualty of the furore over MPs' expenses

On 2 November 2012, Denis MacShane, a former Europe minister under Labour, chose to bring his 18-year parliamentary career to a close in the wake of investigations by the parliamentary standards commissioner and the House of Commons Standards and Privileges Committee that had found his accounts wanting.

The initial complaint that had prompted the investigation, made by a former BNP member, related to invoices that MacShane had submitted in connection with his work travelling in Europe and — as MacShane put it — 'combating racism'. The former minister was also said to have falsely claimed for eight laptops which he had allowed interns to use and then keep between March 2005 and December 2007.

The decision to uphold the BNP complaint against MacShane and recommend that he be suspended from the Commons, without pay or pension rights, for 12 months, left the MP with limited options. MacShane, who readily conceded that his behaviour had been foolish, maintained that he made no personal gain. The police had decided against mounting a prosecution back in July. However, the chair of the standards committee, Kevin Barron, described the case as the 'gravest case which has come before the committee for adjudication' — focusing in particular on the way in which MacShane had opted to submit his invoices through The European Policy Institute, a body that the MP had established in order to fund his trips to other EU states.

Although MacShane's 'foolishness' was less immediately 'obvious' and 'newsworthy' than the John Lewis lists, the duck houses, moat cleaning and 'second-home flipping' of the original MPs' expenses scandal, the case nonetheless highlights the extent to which the ripples from that deep impact are still moving out from the centre. Trust in MPs is proving far harder to re-establish than it was to destroy.

The Leveson Report

Lord Justice Leveson was given the task of investigating 'the culture, practices, and ethics of the press, including...contacts and the relationships between national newspapers and politicians' and 'the press and the police' back in July 2011. His inquiry came in the wake of the phone-hacking scandal that had precipitated the closure of what was then the biggest-selling Sunday newspaper (the *News of the World*). The taking of oral evidence from alleged phone-hacking victims — including the family of murdered school girl Millie Dowler — began in November 2011. A number of alleged and actual perpetrators of the practice were also questioned, along with a veritable Who's Who of leading figures from the worlds of media and Westminster politics. By February 2012 the inquiry had moved on to consider the relationship between the press and the police.

Leveson finally published his 'Report into the culture, practices and ethics of the press' on Thursday, 29 November 2012.

Main findings

The main findings of the Leveson Report were as follows:

- Press behaviour, at times, has been 'outrageous'.
- Politicians and the press have been too close.
- There is no evidence of widespread corruption of the police by the press.
- A new system of self-regulation should be established to oversee the press.
- This new regulatory body should be independent of serving editors, government and business.
- Legislation should be enacted to establish a mechanism to monitor the effectiveness of the new independent regulatory body.
- Government should be placed under a legal duty to protect the freedom of the press.